Stefan Zellmann

Interactive High Performance Volume Rendering

Stefan Zellmann

Interactive High Performance Volume Rendering

Südwestdeutscher Verlag für Hochschulschriften

Impressum / Imprint

Bibliografische Information der Deutschen Nationalbibliothek: Die Deutsche Nationalbibliothek verzeichnet diese Publikation in der Deutschen Nationalbibliografie; detaillierte bibliografische Daten sind im Internet über http://dnb.d-nb.de abrufbar.
Alle in diesem Buch genannten Marken und Produktnamen unterliegen warenzeichen-, marken- oder patentrechtlichem Schutz bzw. sind Warenzeichen oder eingetragene Warenzeichen der jeweiligen Inhaber. Die Wiedergabe von Marken, Produktnamen, Gebrauchsnamen, Handelsnamen, Warenbezeichnungen u.s.w. in diesem Werk berechtigt auch ohne besondere Kennzeichnung nicht zu der Annahme, dass solche Namen im Sinne der Warenzeichen- und Markenschutzgesetzgebung als frei zu betrachten wären und daher von jedermann benutzt werden dürften.

Bibliographic information published by the Deutsche Nationalbibliothek: The Deutsche Nationalbibliothek lists this publication in the Deutsche Nationalbibliografie; detailed bibliographic data are available in the Internet at http://dnb.d-nb.de.
Any brand names and product names mentioned in this book are subject to trademark, brand or patent protection and are trademarks or registered trademarks of their respective holders. The use of brand names, product names, common names, trade names, product descriptions etc. even without a particular marking in this work is in no way to be construed to mean that such names may be regarded as unrestricted in respect of trademark and brand protection legislation and could thus be used by anyone.

Coverbild / Cover image: www.ingimage.com

Verlag / Publisher:
Südwestdeutscher Verlag für Hochschulschriften
ist ein Imprint der / is a trademark of
OmniScriptum GmbH & Co. KG
Heinrich-Böcking-Str. 6-8, 66121 Saarbrücken, Deutschland / Germany
Email: info@svh-verlag.de

Herstellung: siehe letzte Seite /
Printed at: see last page
ISBN: 978-3-8381-5016-1

Zugl. / Approved by: Köln, Universität zu Köln, Diss., 2014

Abstract

This thesis is about Direct Volume Rendering on high performance computing systems. As direct rendering methods do not create a lower-dimensional geometric representation, the whole scientific dataset must be kept in memory. Thus, this family of algorithms has a tremendous resource demand. Direct Volume Rendering algorithms in general are well suited to be implemented for dedicated graphics hardware. Nevertheless, high performance computing systems often do not provide resources for hardware accelerated rendering, so that the visualization algorithm must be implemented for the available general-purpose hardware.

Ever growing datasets that imply copying large amounts of data from the compute system to the workstation of the scientist, and the need to review intermediate simulation results, make porting Direct Volume Rendering to high performance computing systems highly relevant. The contribution of this thesis is twofold.

As part of the first contribution, after devising a software architecture for general implementations of Direct Volume Rendering on highly parallel platforms, parallelization issues and implementation details for various modern architectures are discussed. The contribution results in a highly parallel implementation that tackles several platforms.

The second contribution is concerned with the display phase of the "Distributed Volume Rendering Pipeline". Rendering on a high performance computing system typically implies displaying the rendered result at a remote location. This thesis presents a remote rendering technique that is capable of hiding latency and can thus be used in an interactive environment.

Kurzfassung

Diese Dissertation fokussiert sich auf direktes Volume Rendering auf Höchstleistungs-rechnern. Weil für direkte Visualierungsmethoden keine geometrische Hilfsrepräsen-tation niedrigerer Dimension benötigt wird, so dass der gesamte wissenschaftliche Datensatz im Arbeitsspeicher vorgehalten werden muss, ist der Ressourcenbedarf dieser Familie von Algorithmen immens. Im Allgemeinen bietet sich zur Implemen-tierung eher Grafikhardware an. Diese wird von Höchstleistungsrechnern häufig aber nicht zur Verfügung gestellt, so dass der Visualisierungsalgorithmus speziell für die verfügbare, für den universellen Einsatz gedachte, Hardware implementiert werden muss.

Das stete Wachstum wissenschaftlicher Datensätze impliziert Datenbewegungen im großen Maße vom Höchstleistungsrechner zur Workstation des Wissenschaftlers. Außerdem besteht zunehmend der Bedarf danach, Zwischenergebnisse bereits während der Simulation begutachten zu können. Diese zwei Faktoren begründen die Relevanz dessen, Direktes Volume Rendering für Höchstleistungsrechner zu portieren. Der Beitrag dieser Arbeit ist zu diesem Zwecke zweigeteilt.

Im Rahmen des ersten Teilbeitrags werden auf der Basis einer Software-Architektur-beschreibung, die generelle Implementierungen von Direktem Volume Rendering für hochgradig parallele Plattformen lanciert, Details zur parallelen Implementierung für zahlreiche moderne Architekturen erörtert. Dieser Teilbeitrag resultiert in einer hochgradig parallelen Implementierung, die auf zahlreichen Plattformen effizient lauffähig ist.

Der zweite Teilbeitrag behandelt die Darstellungsphase in der "Verteilten Volume Rendering Pipeline". Rendering auf Höchstleistungsrechnern basiert typischerweise auf Remote Rendering Techniken. Diese Dissertation schlägt eine Remote Rendering Technik vor, mit deren Hilfe es möglich ist, Latenzen zu verstecken, und die deshalb in interaktiven Umgebungen zum Einsatz kommen kann.

Acknowledgements

First and foremost I would like to thank my advisor Prof. Dr. Ulrich Lang. He gave me the opportunity to study an interesting topic in depth. I consider it a privilege. Furthermore, I would like to thank Dr. Jürgen Schulze and the scientists at the High Performance Computing Center Stuttgart (HLRS), who initially developed the DeskVOX volume rendering software. Without their groundwork, this thesis would not have been possible at all.

Special thanks go to my former colleague Martin Aumüller who has been a guide, especially in my first years as a scientist.

My thanks go also to my two student coworkers, Alexander Bolz and Stavros Delisavas. Programming is primarily a lot of work, and much of the work conducted during the course of this thesis would have been left undone without their help.

I also wish to thank my colleagues who read this thesis and who influenced me with their interesting discussions. Their suggestions contributed to the quality of this work. My thanks go, in alphabetical order, to Viktor Achter, Matthias Flasko, and Yvonne Percan.

Some of the figures and results in this thesis are reprints and were originally published by ASME and IASTED, respectively. The original publications are acknowledged at the positions where they occur in the text. The figures were reprinted with friendly permission of the respective copyright owner.

The work for this thesis was conducted over a period of almost five years. During that time, my work was supported by the German Federal Ministry of Education and Research (BMBF), who funded the research project *"Visualization in Parallel Manycore Environments"* (VisPME) [Vis11]. Later, my work was supported by a grant from the Centre for High-Performance Scientific Computing in Terrestrial Systems, HPSC TerrSys, in the Geoverbund ABC/J [HPS12].

Contents

Chapter 1

Introduction

1.1 Structure

This thesis is structured as follows.

Chapter 1, i. e. the remainder of this chapter, outlines the motivation for this thesis. This is followed by a brief overview of the two main contributions presented in this work.

Chapter 2 gives a general overview of scientific visualization algorithms. Being far from comprehensive, this chapter classifies the scientific visualization algorithms that later on are investigated more thoroughly in a broader context.

Chapter 3 summarizes the current state of the art for parallel Direct Volume Rendering algorithms. The problem setting for Direct Volume Rendering along with algorithms to achieve it in real-time is presented. Along with that, parallelization strategies are reviewed that are suitable for different kinds of hardware that is typically found in high performance computing systems.

Chapter 4 devises a software architecture for Distributed Volume Rendering on high performance computing systems. The software architecture follows a pipeline approach. With maximum versatility in mind, the chapter outlines how specialization of various pipeline stages can lead to a visualization tool that is capable of running on highly heterogeneous hardware platforms with manifold usage scenarios ranging from interactive applications in Virtual Reality over in situ visualization to visualization of large datasets on dedicated graphics hardware.

Chapter 5 is concerned with the first major contribution of this thesis and proposes a concrete implementation of the parallel rendering stage of the Distributed Volume Rendering Pipeline introduced in Chapter 4. A sort-last Multi-GPU implementation is accompanied by a CPU-based SIMD implementation, that scales to modern hardware platforms like the Intel® Xeon Phi™ coprocessor. The rendering performance of the system is evaluated.

Chapter 6 elaborates on the second contribution of this work and devises a specific implementation for the display phase of the pipeline from Chapter 4. An interactive technique for remote rendering of volume datasets is presented that allows for hiding latency and computation time by decoupling rendering and display phase. This is achieved by using an image-based rendering technique and 2.5D data from the remote server.

Chapter 7 briefly summarizes the main contributions of this work, reviews its major conclusions and suggests opportunities for future research.

1.2 Motivation

The ubiquity of heterogeneous many-core systems in the recent years not only had an impact on codes that perform scientific calculations, but also on the visualization, which is the predominant part of the ensuing interactive post-processing phase and which is used to gain insights into the scientific data that originates from the simulation. Not only must the visualization algorithms keep pace with the steadily growing dataset sizes that result from scientific simulations, but also with the need of the scientist to explore the simulated data interactively.

In the second half of the last century, high performance computing (HPC) systems were usually used in a batch fashion, i. e. the scientist submitted a compute job, which would later be scheduled for execution and would even later write its results to a mass storage system from which the scientist could retrieve them. While this mode of execution is still the common case in HPC even today, many scientists wish to adapt their simulation at run time based on the inspection of intermediate results. In such scenarios, visualization can help as a means of inspection to create a feedback loop to adapt simulation parameters. Quite often, in such cases it is not desirable or infeasible to copy scientific data from the high performance computing system to the client computer the scientist uses. Designing visualizations that run on the same system as the simulation does can be challenging. On top of that, having to display the data on a computer at a remote location introduces an additional source of overhead and adds heterogeneity to the overall system.

Direct Volume Rendering (DVR) denotes a family of algorithms that can be used to display a wide variety of three-dimensional datasets. Many simulation codes produce results that can be rendered using this family of algorithms or generate outputs that can be resampled to be renderable with DVR. Because of that, it is especially important to adapt DVR algorithms to run on heterogeneous many-core systems, which can be equipped with all types of processors and accelerators.

This thesis illuminates the various aspects that need to be considered when adapting DVR to many-core systems. These aspects include, amongst others, the different parallelization paradigms that the serial algorithms need to be adapted to and considerations for hiding latency introduced by networks connecting the many-core system with the client computer the scientist is interacting with. Theoretical considerations are followed by concrete implementations which are then evaluated regarding their general fitness for the application in terms of the quality of the resulting images, as well as their performance in terms of execution time.

1.3   Contributions

The contribution of this work is divided into two separate areas:

Advances in Parallel Direct Volume Rendering. Modern workstations and HPC systems expose several means for parallelization through add-in card-based coprocessors, programmable GPUs and fast network interconnect. With the advent of GPGPU computing, Multi-GPU systems became prevalent. This work proposes ways to exploit these means for interactive Direct Volume Rendering. Implementations for several modern hardware platforms are evaluated and combined into a flexible software architecture that facilitates Direct Volume Rendering on heterogeneous systems. The developed software is integrated into an open source visualization package and published along with it under an open source software license.

Interactivity Techniques for Remote Volume Rendering. When frame rates drop significantly below 30 Hz, in Virtual Reality this can cause nausea and fatigue. Maintaining interactive frame rates can be a challenge in the context of remote visualization introducing network latency. An image-based interactivity technique for remote rendering is proposed that decouples the rendering phase from the display phase and is thus capable of hiding latency. The decoupling technique is specifically designed for Direct Volume Rendering and relies on heuristics to deduce a depth buffer from volume datasets to generate 2.5D data for remote display.

Chapter 2

Scientific Visualization

The need for visualization can generally arise in any scientific discipline. Natural sciences produce tremendous amounts of data from simulations and measurements. In that case, visualizations are needed that aim at a higher level of *abstraction* to filter the information that is beneficial from the information that doesn't carry any significant meaning. Engineering often aims at the *virtual reconstruction* of tools or machinery, whilst retaining their original proportions, so that they can e. g. be judged regarding *ergonomics*. Archaeologists may have an interest in *physical plausibility*, e. g. when lighting scenarios at ancient sites are simulated in order to understand the original lighting conditions. Artists may be interested in *photorealism*. That said, while the disciplines that develop a need for visualization are manifold, so are the methods that are used to fulfill those needs, and even further, while one type of visualization is suitable for one discipline, it may be counterproductive for the other. This thesis concentrates on visualization scenarios where datasets need to be visualized that are connected to a spatial description, i. e. their underlying topology can be mapped to points in 3D space. Rather than reaching for *photorealism* or *physical plausibility*, the primary aim of the algorithms investigated through the course of this thesis is to distinguish relevant from irrelevant information. Typical fields of application are *medical imaging* or *weather forecasting*. The family of algorithms that this thesis is centered around, *Direct Volume Rendering* (DVR), nevertheless, is not the primary focus of this chapter. Rather than that, this chapter

15

aims at motivating the general notion of scientific visualization, and it tries to devise a formal language to categorize the various types of scientific datasets, along with a broad overview of the general types of algorithms that are applicable to visualize some of those datasets. DVR is a tool that specifically aims at visualizing a certain subset of these datasets.

This introductory chapter is organized as follows. Section 2.1 briefly introduces and defines the notions *visualization* and *scientific visualization*. Section 2.2 provides a formal overview of scientific datasets alongside with a means to classify them regarding their spatial topology and the characteristic traits of the data items that make up the datasets. Section 2.3 reviews pipeline approaches to map data from measurements or simulation to specific visualizations. Section 2.4 gives an overview of some common visualization methods that can be used for the various kinds of datasets, and Section 2.5 gives a short introduction to the connection between scientific visualization and high performance computing (HPC), which is one of the key aspects of this thesis.

2.1   Brief Introduction to Scientific Visualization

Visualization is a discipline that is concerned with the generation of images from general data. McCormick et al. [MDBZ87] define visualization as *"[...] a method of computing (that) [...] transforms the symbolic into the geometric, enabling researchers to observe their simulations and computations. Visualization offers a method for seeing the unseen. It enriches the process of scientific discovery and fosters profound and unexpected insights."* The authors also provided a coarse classification by subdividing visualization into the fields:

- Computer graphics

- Image processing

- Computer vision

- Computer-aided design

- Signal processing

- User interface studies

Hansen and Johnson [JH04] generally described the goal of visualization being *"the creation of a visual representation to help explain complex phenomena"* in their *Visualization Handbook.*

Earnshaw and Wiseman [EW92] postulated that *"Scientific visualization is concerned with exploring data and information in such a way as to gain understanding and insight into the data. The goal of scientific visualization is to promote a deeper level of understanding of the data under investigation and to foster new insight into the underlying processes, relying on the humans' powerful ability to visualize."*

For the purposes of this work, the term scientific visualization will be defined as follows.

Definition 1 (Scientific Visualization) *Scientific visualization is the transformation of abstract data to a geometrical representation in order to gain a further understanding of the data. The need for scientific visualization stems, amongst others, from the humans' limited ability to perceive and imagine N-dimensional problem spaces and aims at narrowing these down to a more comprehensible depiction in the spatial domain of the simulation or the measurement performed to obtain the dataset in the first place. Scientific visualization is often, but not necessarily, aided by computation.*

This working definition expresses several aspects in which the author's opinion differs from those of the authors of the aforementioned textbooks.

In contrast to McCormick et al., the author argues that visualization is not solely a method of computing but in general the result of human imagination, independent of the medium the individual uses to express his or her imagination.

This work's definition differs from that of Earnshaw and Wiseman in that it specifically does not state information as the entity to be visualized. Underlying this is a distinction between the notions *data* and *information* which assumes that data is uninterpreted. Raw data can however be converted to meaningful information through a cognitive process. In fact, the author argues that the process of visualizing data is one that actually facilitates this very transformation of abstract data to information, which is then accessible and useful to the scientist. This distinction is also reasonable in order to distinguish the field of scientific visualization from the large field of *information visualization*, which is not covered by this work. Scientific datasets are typically located in a spatial domain like in 2D or 3D space. In that case, the spatial context does not need to be deduced but is present *a priori*, which is in contrast to the datasets that are typically processed using information visualization.

For multi-dimensional datasets, i. e. datasets which may have an underlying spatial topology but exhibit single data items with a higher dimensionality than that of the space they are located in, the best mapping needs to be found that extracts the most relevant information regarding the parts of the data items pertaining to the remaining dimensions. Narrowing down the data to depict the relevant information in a perceivable way is of uttermost importance. Examples of multi-dimensional datasets can be found in turbulence simulation, where the simulation domain spans a spatial context and data items consist e. g. of velocity vectors in conjunction with pressure and particle emission. Visualizing multi-dimensional datasets can be accomplished by combining several of the techniques that are all but briefly motivated in Section 2.4.

2.2   Classification of Scientific Datasets

Scientific visualization methods are designed to explore various types of datasets differing in terms of their underlying *topology*, their *dimensionality* and their *time dependence*. In the following, a mathematical formalism to classify scientific datasets in terms of those properties is introduced.

In general, scientific datasets are made up of a finite set of *data items*, which are located in an $N-dimensional$ Hilbert space. The topology of the dataset determines the connectivity of these data items in space *and* time. Specific manifestations of topologies are e. g. *scattered* topologies [CJ05], *grid* topologies [HLC91] or *mesh*

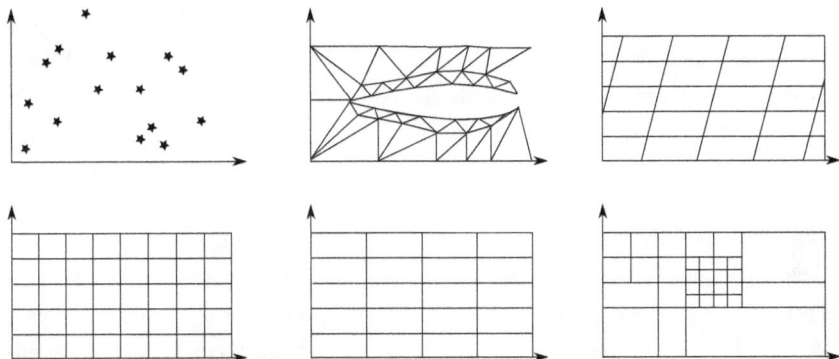

Figure 2.1: Topologies with varying degree of structuredness. From left to right, Top to bottom: scattered data, structured grid, regular grid, cartesian grid with equidistant spacing between vertices, rectilinear grid with equidistant spacing between vertices in each dimension, adaptive grid structure where nodes with a higher resolution emphasize regions of interest.

topologies [TYRG+06]. Grid topologies impose a cyclic, closed graph data structure on top of the dataset, where the locations of the data items are modeled as vertices and connections are modeled as edges. Grid topologies can be further classified into *structured* and *unstructured* grids, where structure implies a regular pattern of the connections between the data items regarding distances between vertices and angles between edges. In cases where the number of edges leaving a vertex cell is constant, one often refers to grid topologies in terms of the $N - dimensional$ geometric primitive the edges connecting neighboring vertices form, resulting in terms like *rectangular* grids or *tetrahedron* grids. The volumetric regions spanned by the convex hull of these geometric primitives are referred to as *cells*. Figure 2.1 shows numerous examples of 2D topologies exhibiting varying degrees of structuredness. A good overview of topologies for scientific datasets is given in Chapter 7 of [JH04].

The dimensionality of scientific datasets on the one hand depends on the dimensionality of the Hilbert space the data items are located in. On the other hand, the dimensionality depends on the domain of the data items. Specialized scientific visualization methods exist for 2D and 3D spatial dimensions and for data items such as *scalars*, *vectors* or *tensors* [HPvW94].

Time dependent datasets typically exhibit time-varying data items. The topology of
the dataset may also vary with time. This may have a varying impact on the way
the dataset is stored and processed. Regular, adaptive grid topologies are used when
the researcher exploring the dataset is especially interested in specific regions that
are modeled using a higher grid resolution than the rest of the spatial domain. If
these regions of interest are in motion, it may be possible to store the change of the
grid with time as an *increment* of the previous time step and not having to store the
whole topology anew for each frame. With unstructured grids, storing increments in
general may be more difficult because of the weak connectivity of arbitrary grid cells.
Anyhow, the dimensionality of scientific datasets that this thesis focuses on usually
does not vary with time.

In accordance to this classification, a general way to analytically describe scientific
datasets is by using tuples of the form (X, S, T), where X denotes the topology of
the dataset, S stands for the data value at the grid position that depends on the
dimensionality of the domain and $T \in \mathbb{N} \setminus 0$ denotes time dependence.

For example, the tuple

$$((i, j, k), s),\tag{2.1}$$

$i, j, k \in \mathbb{N}$, describes a 3D dataset located on a uniform grid, where each grid cell
stores a scalar value and the dataset consists of only one time step.

The tuple

$$((x_i, x_j), (v_x, v_y), t),\tag{2.2}$$

$x_i, x_j \in \mathbb{R}$, $i, j \in \mathbb{N}$ can be used to express a dataset located on an unstructured grid,
with multiple time steps storing vectors at each cell.

This mathematically formal description can be used to *generally* describe each type of
the scientific datasets that the algorithms elaborated upon in this thesis are applicable
to. In terms of a formal definition, the dataset is then a *function* of *space* and *time*,

which maps to a single variable or a higher dimensional codomain. Apart from that, this formal description makes no assumptions on how *actual values* of the function can be retrieved. For most nontrivial datasets, an analytical description is impossible to find. Datasets from measurement or simulation are usually available as a *set of tuples* for each specific data item. That said, in that case, it is the very nature of the dataset that there is a tuple for *every* data item in space, and for high resolutions of the underlying topology of the dataset, the amount of tuples can be tremendous. Because of that, apart from the formal description of a dataset in a mathematical sense, one also needs to consider the way that actual data items are stored, and the amount of data items that need to be visualized strongly influences the visualization algorithms that are applicable for the dataset. This thesis concentrates on algorithms that can cope with large grids that store tremendous amounts of data items.

2.3 Visualization Pipelines

In order to visualize datasets like the ones described above, post-processing steps are necessary to generate images from the abstract data items. Visualization pipelines often constitute the principal ground on which visualization systems are built. Frequently, the dataflow through the visualization pipeline is visually programmable e. g. by using a dataflow network. Examples of visualization software packages that facilitate this type of visual programming are ParaView (cf. Section 3.5.4)

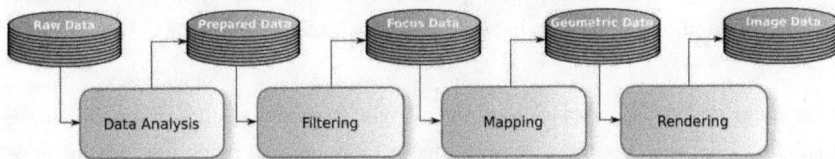

Figure 2.2: Haber McNabb visualization pipeline, enhanced with a data analysis phase as proposed by dos Santos and Brodlie. The data analysis stage is typically not interactive and is used to transition from multivariate or multidimensional data to data that can be visualized, e. g. by means of interpolation or a Principal Component Analysis.

and COVISE (cf. Section 3.5.6). Haber and McNabb [HM90] proposed a dataflow model that datasets must be subjected to in order to create displayable content. The pipeline comprises the stages

Filtering. During filtering, raw data is filtered for items of interest. When e. g. the turbulent flow of water in a drainage system is simulated, sites like crossings or bends may be of higher interest because phenomena like eddies are likely to occur there, while plane bendings may be less interesting and are thus not considered for visualization. The filtering stage is often user controlled. The data after filtering is called *focus data*.

Mapping. The mapping stage assigns positional information and properties like colors to the focus data from filtering. Often, the mapping step is actually a *remapping* step, e. g. if the original data was simulated on a rectangular grid, and is replaced with a hierarchical data structure that carries the same information but can be rendered more efficiently. The *geometric data* that results from this pipeline stage must be in a form that is e. g. suitable for one or a combination of the visualization algorithms described in Section 2.4.

Rendering. At this stage, an actual image is created from the geometric representation that was obtained during mapping. Rendering is often hardware accelerated. Then, the implementation of the algorithm that is used must be capable of producing graphic primitives that are supported by the graphics hardware. As a result of this pipeline stage, image data in the form of pixels is generated, that can e. g. be written to the frame buffer.

One might argue that in some cases, the mapping step is obsolete or there is no clear distinction between mapping and filtering or mapping and rendering. For instance, if the simulation was performed on a grid in the first place, and this grid is now reused for rendering, a mapping to geometric data is unnecessary. On the other hand, post-classification transfer functions (cf. Section 2.4.4) map data values to colors after reconstruction, which is typically performed during rendering. Also, if hierarchical data structures are employed for filtering, e. g. to put a higher emphasize on certain regions of interest and assigning more grid cells to those than to other regions, filtering actually implies a geometric mapping.

In 2004, dos Santos and Brodlie [dSB04] enhanced this model with a data analysis phase to address multidimensional data (cf. Figure 2.2). Dasgupta and Kosara [DK12] added a feedback loop to the visualization pipeline that is based on cognition and perception and that can be used to alter parameters of the various stages to adapt the rendered output dynamically. In general, the various stages of the pipeline are often implemented to be adapted interactively. For example, the process of finding an appropriate location for a cutting surface is a user controlled filtering step. The ensuing process of finding an appropriate mapping e. g. from densities to colors is also often guided through user interaction, and during rendering the user usually interacts with the dataset by adjusting camera parameters like view point and zoom. If the user is not satisfied with the result, she may return to any of the pipeline stages and make adjustments.

2.4 Visualization Methods for Scientific Datasets

This section introduces some of the more commonly used methods to visualize scientific datasets. As there is an overwhelming variety of visualization methods applicable to the numerous kinds of datasets described above, this section only presents a small, representative selection of visualization algorithms. The section mainly focuses on visualization methods aimed at 3D datasets with an underlying grid topology. The family of DVR algorithms, which also falls under this category, will be covered in more detail in Chapter 3 and is thus omitted from this section.

2.4.1 Contouring

Contouring algorithms extract isolines from 2D datasets or isosurfaces from 3D datasets. Contours are extracted by defining an *isovalue* that falls in the range of possible data values and which is used to determine which data items are on the inside or on the outside of the contour. Generally speaking, given a dataset

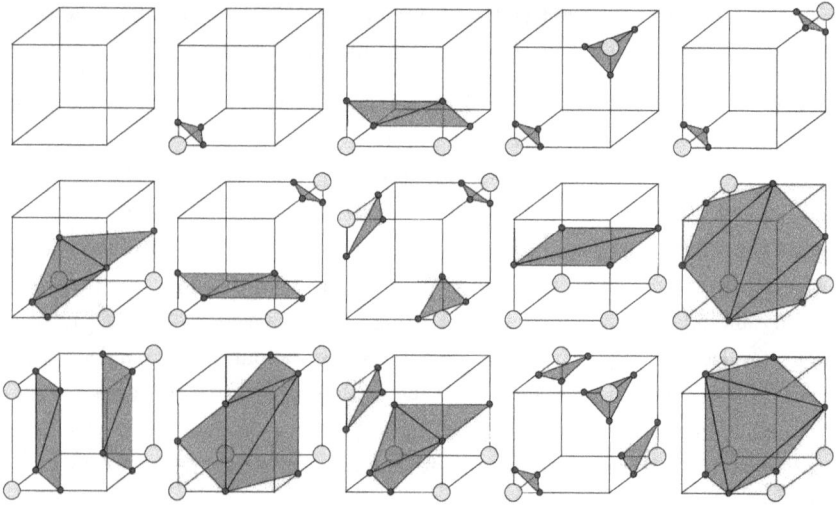

Figure 2.3: Marching cubes contouring algorithm: the patterns are used to derive the 256 possible ways an isosurface may intersect a box through permutation.

(X, S, T), contouring algorithms hence extract only those parts of the dataset where S takes on a specific value $c \in S$, for arbitrary X and arbitrary T. In the 3D case, the contour then represents the infinitesimally thin transition between two different media. Contours are typically extracted as part of an offline process and are then converted e. g. to a polygon mesh that can be rendered with graphic acceleration. The Marching Cubes Algorithm [LC87] is a famous representative of the family of contouring algorithms for the 3D case. An isosurface is extracted by independently processing the cuboid cells of a uniform 3D grid. The eight data values at the vertices of each cuboid are evaluated to be on the inside or on the outside of the isosurface using the isovalue. If one of two neighboring vertices is on the inside and the other one is on the outside, the exact location where the isosurface intersects the connecting edge is approximated using linear interpolation. Only a limited edge configuration can possibly be intersected by the isosurface, so that the triangulation for each configuration, that is necessary for edge generation, can efficiently be stored in a lookup table. All 256 possible cases can then be obtained as a permutation of one of the 15 patterns depicted in Figure 2.3. Unit normals are necessary for shading calculations. These are obtained by calculating central differences for the box vertices. From these, normals for the triangle vertices can also be calculated using linear interpolation.

2.4.2 Slicing

Slicing or *cutting* in general is a process that extracts a lower order representation from a higher order representation by leaving out information. Slicing algorithms are quite often combined with a facility for *probing*, which requires the visualization algorithm to run interactively and enables finding an appropriate location e. g. of a 3D cutting geometry through user interaction. Generally, in a common slicing scenario a dataset (X, S, T) is given, with arbitrary X, S and T. Further a *proxy representation* (Y, T) is given. The algorithm then proceeds by extracting only those values from the original dataset for visualization where $x = y$, $x \in X$ and $y \in Y$. This is usually followed by a mapping process to colorize the extracted data, e. g. by using contouring (cf. Section 2.4.1) or color mapping (cf. Section 2.4.4). Quite often, (Y, T) is a plain represented through a normal $N \in Y$ and an anchor position $P \in Y$, and $Y = \mathbb{R}^3$. It is safe to say that the most common usage scenario of slicing algorithms is one where $X = \mathbb{R}^3$ and $Y = \mathbb{R}^3$, i. e. information is extracted from a 3D dataset using a 3D *cutting surface*. In contrast to contouring, where information was extracted based upon evaluating S to have taken on a certain value, slicing algorithms extract information based on spatial location X.

2.4.3 Particle Tracing

Yet another family of visualization algorithms is *particle tracing*, where the aim is to extract information that is related to the progression of data items over time $t \in T$. Particle tracing is used to extract *trajectories* from *vector fields*. Generally, datasets of the type (X, S, T), where $t \in T > 1$, can be meaningfully used to perform particle tracing. Furthermore, most often $S \in \mathbb{R}^3$ is a vector space that represents velocity. Particles are then *released* into the velocity *vector field* at positions $y_t \in Y, t \in T$. The initial positions are called *seed points*. If $y_t \in X$, y is *subjected* by the vector field and a new position y_{t+1} is computed using integration. The integration order will directly influence the fitness of the position estimate. Fourth order integration like it is performed using the *Runge-Kutta method* [Bak77] has proven to provide stable computational results. Particle tracing algorithms can be distinguished based upon the way that actual trajectories are depicted over the course of time. *Pathlines* show the whole paths that particles follow after being released into the vector field, until eventually leaving it. *Streamlines* represent only the local orientation of particles in an instance of time. Most recently, with the advent of general-purpose programming capabilities of GPUs, particle tracing implementations have become feasible [Bus11] that allow not only for interactively setting seed points, but also for interactive trajectory computation.

2.4.4   Color Mapping

Color mapping provides a means to express certain information by assigning color to specific properties of data items. In case of simple color maps, a color is provided for a specific data value using a lookup table. The data values are usually scalar to obtain reasonable sizes for the lookup table.

Quite often, a general mapping

$$t : D \to \mathbb{R}^c \tag{2.3}$$

from the data domain D to a visual spectrum $\mathbb{R}^c$ is desired. Most often, the spectrum is represented by a color space like RGB, so that a common case implies that $c = 3$. Such functions, which map data values to colors are called *transfer functions*. Since the mapped colors are not useful on their own but depend on a proxy representation, transfer functions are used in conjunction e. g. with one of the visualization methods introduced in this section. In the case of slicing, it usually suffices or is even desirable to only map from data values to colors.

In the context of Direct Volume Rendering algorithms, which this thesis is focused on and which are the gist of the ensuing chapter, on top of that, a mapping

$$t : D \to \mathbb{R} \qquad (2.4)$$

from data values to transparency is desirable in addition to mere color mapping. In addition to that, there is in general no restriction regarding which kind of data should be mapped to colors or transparency. In the presence of *fields*, e. g. the *gradient* may be a trait of interest that can be mapped and can provide further insight at regions where different media transition.

Some visualization algorithms like slicing or Direct Volume Rendering rely e. g. on trilinear or higher-order interpolation to reconstruct the dataset between grid cells. Transfer functions can then be applied *pre-interpolative*, i. e. to the actual data items of the grid, or *post-interpolative*, i. e. to the interpolated data sample. Since transfer function application is often referred to as *classification*, the classification order is often referred to using the terms *pre-classification* and *post-classification*. Hadwiger et al. show in Chapter 4 of [HKRS⁺06], that post-interpolative transfer functions are better suited for reconstruction of datasets containing high frequencies.

Transfer function design, specifically in conjunction with DVR, is a research topic on its own because the task of finding a useful mapping from a field to colors and opacities tends to be challenging for users, that typically are no computer scientists, but rather surgeons or neurologists, which rely on transfer functions to distinguish e. g. a tumor from healthy tissue. *Automatic transfer function design* [KD98] [ZT09] [RBB⁺11] can be useful if a bulk of datasets is processed or if for any other reason a thorough review of each dataset through the user is impractical or not possible at all. Quite often, the default transfer function used in visualization systems is the rainbow color map, which maps data items to highly saturated colors. Alternatives were proposed which also take perceptual considerations into account [Mor09].

2.5 Scientific Visualization and High Performance Computing

Scientific visualization and HPC are interdependent in that on the one hand, visualization is typically the predominant step of the interactive post-processing phase of simulations, and on the other hand because it relies on resources that allow for interactive computation of the algorithms involved in visualization. With an increase in the compute resources that are available for visualization, parts of the visualization pipeline outlined above can be implemented interactively, which was impossible so far. For example, with the advent of general-purpose computing capabilities on GPUs (see Section 3.3.4), contouring algorithms or particle tracing can be computed in real-time under certain conditions [Bus11] [AW13]. With GPUs becoming available as cluster resources, and graphics researchers using programming paradigms like message passing or multithreading, the interdependence between the two disciplines grows to an even higher degree. Under these conditions, concepts to optimize the communication patterns during post-processing need to be iterated. If e. g. significant parts of the visualization pipeline are performed on an HPC system, remote rendering (cf. Chapter 6) can be employed, and bandwidth issues must be taken into consideration. *In situ visualization* is a concept that aims at providing a feedback loop to interactively monitor intermediary results in order to adjust parameters of an ongoing simulation.

From the development of the recent years, it seems clear that the two disciplines, scientific visualization and high performance computing, must be considered in conjunction rather than as two separate research areas. The book edited by Bethel et al. [BCH12] provides a general overview of the concepts involved when intermingling the realm of scientific visualization with that of HPC. Many of the concepts introduced there, like e. g. sort-last compositing, are highly relevant for this thesis. In contrast to being general about mixing scientific visualization and HPC, this thesis focuses on Direct Volume Rendering specifically. The ensuing chapter focuses on the current state of the art in Direct Volume Rendering on HPC systems. While Chapter 4 devises a software architecture for volume rendering on HPC systems, concrete implementations are proposed and evaluated in Chapters 5 and 6.

Chapter 3

State of the Art in Parallel Direct Volume Rendering

Section 2.2 proposed a notation to describe scientific datasets as a function of their topology, their dimensionality and their time dependence. Some subset from the huge selection of available algorithms for scientific visualization was introduced that is applicable to various kinds of scientific datasets.

The following section concentrates on a set of algorithms that are used to implement one specific visualization technique called Direct Volume Rendering (DVR). That technique is used to *directly* render datasets of the general form

$$(X, S, T), \ X \in \mathbb{R}^3, \ S \in \mathbb{R}^n \ and \ T \in \mathbb{N}. \tag{3.1}$$

Direct rendering in this case means that a direct mapping from the data domain to the image plane is preferred over e. g. *explicitly* extracting a representative geometry like an isosurface first and rendering that afterwards. Although DVR is applicable to general grid topologies, and although algorithms like e. g. ray casting (see Section 3.2.6) in its general form or cell projection (see Section 3.2.5) specifically support unstructured grid types, the datasets of interest in this thesis typically are of the form

$$(X, S, T), \ X \in \mathbb{N}^3, \ S \in \mathbb{R} \ and \ T \in \mathbb{N}. \tag{3.2}$$

Note that hierarchical grid types can be completely described by combining uniform grids using a *divide and conquer* strategy. Uniform grids and their hierarchical "siblings" typically originate from medical imaging methods such as magnet resonance tomography (MRT) or X-ray computed tomography (CT), or from simulations like the ones used in astrophysics or meteorology.

This chapter begins with a description of the physical phenomena involved when light interacts with participating media in a volume of space, resulting in an integral equation (the *scattering equation*), that DVR algorithms seek to solve incrementally. In the following, the current state of the art in sequential DVR algorithms is presented. This is followed by a brief recapitulation of the general parallel programming models that are used to optimize for different hardware platforms. Then a description follows on how these programming models can be used to parallelize the various sequential DVR algorithms. The chapter concludes with an overview of actual DVR implementations that can be found in current visualization systems.

3.1   Introduction to Direct Volume Rendering

The following section provides the reader with an introduction to the kind of problems solved with Direct Volume Rendering, as well as with a brief overview of how DVR is typically implemented on modern hardware. A more comprehensive overview of methods for real-time DVR and their theoretical background can e. g. be found in the textbook by Hadwiger et al. [HKRS+06]. This section on the optical models underlying DVR is loosely based upon this textbook, as well as on the paper by Max [Max95] and the chapter on DVR and transfer function pre-integration from the Visualization Handbook [JH04].

DVR is a visualization technique that is typically used to display 3D fields. The data items at each discrete location of the 3D field are often, but not necessarily, scalars. The topology of the 3D field is expressed through a 3D grid. DVR in its

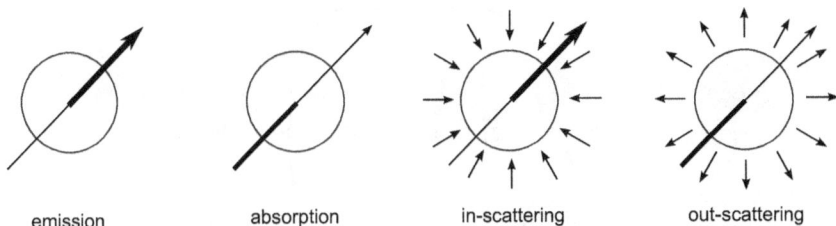

emission   absorption   in-scattering   out-scattering

Figure 3.1: Phenomena involved in the interaction of light traveling along a ray, and the matter that is contained by the medium that the ray travels through. The depiction is inspired by Figure 1.3 from Hadwiger et al. [HKRS+06]. Emission of radiative energy is due to heat that originates from light interacting with matter. Absorption is the opposite phenomenon, where radiative energy is transformed into heat. Scattering phenomena are usually evaluated probabilistically and also result in energy associated with the light ray being increased or removed.

general form is used interdisciplinarily, with applications coming e. g. from medicine, engineering or natural sciences. As stated in [BCH12], DVR algorithms generate images from volume data without explicit geometry extraction. Although being computationally more expensive, direct rendering methods prevent information loss. On top of that, parameters like isovalues, since being applied to the data directly, are typically implemented using table lookups and thus do not impose execution halts e. g. for extracting a new isosurface.

DVR methods aim to solve the scattering equation [KVH84]. The scattering equation stems from geometric optics and provides a physically approximate basis to describe the interaction of light and matter from the participating medium that light is traveling through. This is typically expressed in terms of the following phenomena (cf. Figure 3.1) that light running along a straight line interacting with matter is subject to.

Emission. A heated body emits radiation, and some of the emitted radiative energy possibly falls in the frequency of visible light.

Absorption. Radiative energy that can be encountered along the light ray interacts with the medium and is converted to heat.

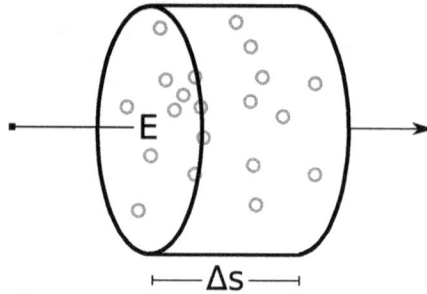

Figure 3.2: Schematic that physically motivates the light-matter interaction models introduced in this section. In the limit, when Δs goes to 0, absorption, emission and scattering become proportional to the projected area of the particles.

In-Scattering. Radiative energy from the medium is scattered towards the light ray, resulting in an increased amount of energy associated with the ray.

Out-Scattering. Radiation that is located along the path of the light ray is scattered towards the outside of the participating medium. Thus, energy is removed from the ray.

The following mathematical formulation of the aforementioned phenomena that eventually results in a construct called the *volume rendering integral* is based on Max 1995 [Max95] and Section 8.1 of [JH04], which is basically a summary of the aforementioned publication.

The probability of light being emitted, absorbed or scattered along a ray is in the following considered to be proportional to the amount of particles ρ per unit volume along the direction ω of the ray. Particles are considered to be spherical with projected area $A = \pi r^2$. The particles flow through a cylinder having a base of area E and a length of Δs. Thus the cylinder contains $N = \rho E \Delta s$ particles per unit of time t (cf. Figure 3.2).

Let Δs now tend to 0. Then, in a model that takes *only absorption* into account, the light intensity gathered along the ray at distance s is described by the differential equation

$$\frac{dI}{ds} = -\tau(s) I(s), \tag{3.3}$$

which can be analytically solved as follows:

$$I(s) = I_0 e^{-\int_0^s \tau(t)dt}. \tag{3.4}$$

I_0 denotes the light intensity at $s = 0$, i. e. the position where the ray enters the volume, and $\tau = A\rho$ denotes the *extinction coefficient*.

The term that I_0 is multiplied with,

$$T(s) = e^{-\int_0^s \tau(t)dt}, \tag{3.5}$$

is called the *transparency* at position s. The *absorption only* model thus describes the influence of the medium at each continuous position s acting upon a background light source.

Assuming that the particles now glow diffusely and letting Δs go to 0 again, the *emission only* model can be described by the differential equation

$$\frac{dI}{ds} = C(s) \rho(s) A = C(s) \tau(s) = g(s), \tag{3.6}$$

with the *source term* $g(s)$ accounting for *glow* that adds energy scattered towards the eye along the direction of the ray. Solving this differential equation yields

$$I(s) = I_0 + \int_0^s g(t) \, dt. \tag{3.7}$$

Combining the two models yields the *absorption plus emission* model

$$\frac{dI}{ds} = g(s) - \tau(s) I(s) \tag{3.8}$$

and its analytical solution

$$I\left(s\right) = I_0 e^{-\int_0^s \tau(r)dr} + \int_0^s g\left(t\right) e^{-\int_t^s \tau(r)dr} dt. \tag{3.9}$$

In this model, the background light is attenuated, and emitted energy is scattered towards the eye. The emitted energy is then itself attenuated by the opacity that was already *gathered* along the ray so far.

In addition to emission and absorption, *external illumination* is usually accounted for by evaluating a local shading formula such as the *Lambert* formula for diffuse or the *Phong* formula for specular lighting [Pho75] at positions where the ray interacts with the medium. The normal needed to evaluate such lighting models is usually approximated by calculating the gradient $\nabla f\left(x, y, z\right)$. The gradient for an *arbitrary position* in the medium is usually estimated by using central differences in a region $[f\left(x, y, z\right) - \delta, f\left(x, y, z\right) + \delta]$, i. e.

$$\nabla f\left(x, y, z\right) = \frac{1}{2\delta} \begin{pmatrix} f\left(x+\delta, y, z\right) + f\left(x-\delta, y, z\right) \\ f\left(x, y+\delta, z\right) + f\left(x, y-\delta, z\right) \\ f\left(x, y, z+\delta\right) + f\left(x, y, z-\delta\right) \end{pmatrix} \tag{3.10}$$

(cf. [HKRS+06], Section 5.3).

Local illumination is then calculated at position X as

$$S\left(X, \omega\right) = r\left(X, \omega, \omega'\right) i\left(X, \omega'\right), \tag{3.11}$$

where $r\left(X, \omega, \omega'\right)$ is a *bidirectional reflection distribution function* (BRDF), $i\left(X, \omega'\right)$ is the incoming light intensity at position x from direction ω', and ω is the direction into which light is reflected.

Local illumination usually only contributes if the gradient magnitude is well defined at the respective sampling position. Otherwise, the local illumination term is set to 0 and only emission and absorption are accounted for.

Local illumination is combined with the emission and absorption model by adjusting the source term g from above to account for non-directional glow $E(X)$ *and* the single-scattering term $S(X, \omega, \omega')$:

$$g(X, \omega) = E(X) + S(X, \omega) \tag{3.12}$$

More complicated models adjust the source term g to account for multiple scattering as well. Evaluating multiple scattering involves finding the intensity at *each* position x in *each* direction ω, so that the source term at distance s becomes

$$g(s, \omega) = \int_{4\pi} r(X = s\omega, \omega, \omega') I(X - s\omega, \omega') \, d\omega', \tag{3.13}$$

which integrates the incoming light from all directions on the unit sphere. Only more recent publications concentrate on producing images accounting for multiple scattering in real-time [ASW13] [ZM13], while typical real-time implementations incorporated into popular visualization systems (cf. Section 3.5) usually only account for emission, absorption and local illumination at best.

Because there exists no analytical solution to the scattering equation for nontrivial datasets, the problem is usually discretized e. g. by substituting a Riemann sum for the integration. Consider the absorption plus emission model represented through Equation 3.8. The integral underneath the continuous curve representing the extinction coefficient $\tau(s)$ can be approximated using a sum:

$$\int_0^s \tau(r) \, dr \approx \sum_{i=1}^n \tau(i\Delta x) \, \Delta x, \tag{3.14}$$

where $\Delta x = \frac{D}{n}$ is the step size and n is the number of steps necessary to march a ray from the outermost edge of the volume at position 0 to the eye at position D.

Further, from the rule of exponents it follows that

$$e^{-\sum_{i=1}^{n} \tau(i\Delta x)\Delta x} = \prod_{i=1}^{n} e^{-\tau(i\Delta x)\Delta x}. \tag{3.15}$$

Similar considerations hold for the rest of Equation 3.8, which can then approximately be solved using the following system of Riemann summations:

$$I(D) \approx I_0 \prod_{i=1}^{n} t_i + \sum_{i=1}^{n} g_i \prod_{j=i+1}^{n} t_j, \tag{3.16}$$

where $t_i = e^{\tau(i\Delta x)}$ and $g_i = g(i\Delta x)$.

Applying some further transformations and letting $\alpha_{src} = 1 - T(s)$ (i. e. reformulating Equation 3.16 in terms of opacity rather than transparency), this yields the basic operation that is necessary to compose an image from a discretized version of the scattering equation: alpha compositing. The compositing equations provide calculation rules to derive color and opacity based on the order in which volume samples are blended to form a final image. The compositing equations apply to all of the DVR algorithms described in Section 3.2. They are independent of the type of decomposition that the algorithm requires to evaluate the scattering equation - some of the algorithms rely on an image space decomposition, while others rely on an object space decomposition. Nevertheless, depending on the traversal order in which e. g. a ray or a slicing plain is traversed through the volume, either the front-to-back compositing equation

$$\begin{aligned} C_{dst} &= C_{dst} + (1 - \alpha_{dst})\,\alpha_{src}C_{src} \\ \alpha_{dst} &= \alpha_{dst} + (1 - \alpha_{dst})\,\alpha_{src} \end{aligned} \tag{3.17}$$

or the back-to-front compositing equation

$$\begin{aligned} C_{dst} &= \alpha_{src}C_{src} + (1 - \alpha_{src})\,C_{dst} \\ \alpha_{dst} &= \alpha_{src} + (1 - \alpha_{src})\,\alpha_{dst} \end{aligned} \tag{3.18}$$

applies, where C_{src} is the color portion of the incoming radiance, C_{dst} is the radiance that was already accumulated, α_{src} is the opacity associated with the sampling position and α_{dst} is the accumulated opacity.

The relationship between the two compositing equations, which are also referred to as the *under*-operator (front-to-back) and *over*-operator (back-to-front) [PD84], and the emission and absorption model can also be seen by representing the exponential from Equation 3.4 as a Taylor series expansion:

$$I\left(s\right) = I_0 e^{-\int_0^s \tau(t)dt} = I_0 \left(1 - \tau\left(s\right) + \frac{(\tau s)^2}{2!} - \frac{(\tau s)^3}{3!} + \dots\right) \approx I_0\left(1 - \tau\left(s\right)\right) \quad (3.19)$$

(cf. Section 8.2.1.2 of [JH04]), which corresponds to accounting for absorption by multiplying C_{dst} and α_{dst} by $(1 - \alpha_{src})$.

When accumulating opacity by e. g. marching a ray through the volume density using Equations 3.17 or 3.18 to evaluate the sums from equation 3.16, the *sampling frequency* n must be chosen appropriately (i. e. according to the sampling theorem, see e. g. [FvDFH90] and the remarks regarding pre-integrated classification below). Anyway, for the time being, consider n to be chosen arbitrarily, e. g. based on a performance measurement that is used to maintain a certain, fixed frame rate at run time and adjusts n accordingly. Because n directly affects the ray marching step size D/n, decreasing n will result in the overall opacity to decrease because the extinction coefficient is obtained through a transfer function lookup, and the result from that lookup is absolute rather than relative to the step size. This is reasonable regarding a continuous integration but will result in inconsistencies with Riemann summation. Then an opacity correction step that adjusts the absolute opacity to the step size is necessary [LCNC98] [KLT07]:

$$\alpha' = 1 - \sqrt[n]{1 - \alpha}. \quad (3.20)$$

Alternative compositing schemes not based on the scattering equation exist. Maximum intensity projection (MIP) [HMS95], which is e. g. used for X-ray imaging, assigns the color of the volume sample with the highest intensity:

$$C_{dst} = max \left\{ C_{dst}, C_{src} \right\}.$$ (3.21)

This compositing scheme in general is less computationally intensive because there is no need to sort for front-to-back or back-to-front evaluation (neglecting bandwidth considerations that possibly mandate a coherent traversal order). On the other hand, by neglecting the traversal order when weighing the volume samples encountered during volume traversal, natural depth cues are not accounted for, that would otherwise result from attenuation through volume density in front of the current sample. While the focus of this thesis is on DVR algorithms that employ alpha compositing, adapting to alternative compositing schemes like MIP can be implemented intuitively by substituting only a few calculations, especially if the alternative compositing scheme is order-independent.

Deciding for one of the two traversal orders has certain implications concerning the reliability of the final image as well as on optimization opportunities that exist for certain algorithms. Given that the discretized evaluation of the scattering equation is performed with limited floating-point precision, the result obtained through front-to-back compositing will in general be different from the result obtained through back-to-front compositing. This is because the addition operation $(+)$ and the multiplication operation $(\times)$ for floating-point numbers in general do not have the associative property. Because of the iterative nature of the two compositing equations, round-off errors will grow more severe because of accumulation. With the front-to-back compositing scheme, samples near the viewing position will affect the final image to a higher degree, while it is the other way around with back-to-front compositing. The influence of the round-off errors will increase with increasing sampling rates. Front-to-back compositing can facilitate the implementation of the early-ray termination optimization strategy (cf. e. g. [MIH04]).

Engel et al. [EKE01] proposed to enhance DVR using a technique called *pre-integrated classification*. From the sampling theorem follows that a signal can only be reconstructed if it is band-limited and if sampling frequencies higher than the

Nyquist frequency, i. e. twice the frequency of the original signal, are used for sampling [FvDFH90]. However, if the term $\tau(s)$ from Equation 3.8 is obtained from a transfer function, reconstruction of the original signal results in not only having to sample the 3D volume data, but also the transfer function which potentially contains high frequencies too. With the naive approach, the appropriate sampling frequency is proportional to the Nyquist frequency of the volume *times* the Nyquist frequency of the transfer function. With pre-integration, however, opacity as a function of two sample positions s_1 and s_2 and the length of the line segment spanning s_1 and s_2 is pre-calculated and then stored in a lookup table. This lookup table is then used instead of the post-classification lookup that would usually have been performed. That way, the appropriate sampling frequency is only proportional to the frequency of the volume dataset. Pre-integrating the transfer function thus helps to reduce round-off errors and to increase performance because of the lower sampling frequency necessary. Pre-integrated classification in general is applicable to each of the DVR algorithms motivated in the following section.

3.2 Direct Volume Rendering Algorithms

An interactive solution to the scattering equation laid out in the previous section is only possible to obtain for trivial problems. In more realistic cases, a trade off is necessary between interactivity and the physical correctness of the output image. Interactive DVR algorithms often only take the absorption and emission term of the scattering equation into account. Scattering phenomena are often simplified to single-scattering only. Figure 3.3 shows a medical dataset obtained from a computed tomography that is rendered using DVR and local illumination with the Blinn-Phong reflectance model [Bli77].

The following subsections summarize algorithms for interactive DVR. Being designed to target different hardware platforms, these algorithms are part of visualization systems that are widely used by researchers. Each algorithm either relies on a decomposition of the volume dataset in object space or on a decomposition of image space for display.

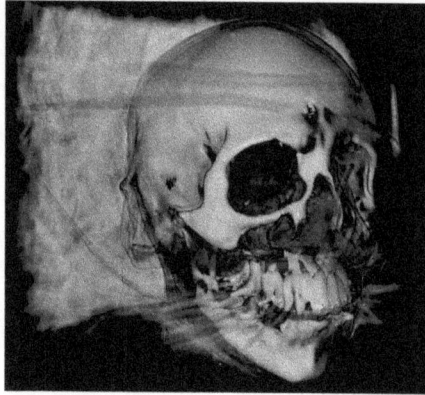

Figure 3.3: Computed tomography medical dataset rendered using DVR, with a local illumination model applied.

3.2.1   Texture-Based Volume Rendering

Texture-based Direct Volume Rendering algorithms are specifically designed for hardware with texture mapping capabilities like GPUs or dedicated graphic workstations. The first authors to propose texture-based DVR algorithms were Hastreiter et al. [HÇE96] and later Westermann and Ertl [WE98] or Dachille et al. [DKC+98]. Krüger et al. [KW03] provided an overview of how to implement texture-based approaches on modern GPUs. A thorough overview can also be found in the aforementioned textbook by Hadwiger et al. [HKRS+06].

Texture-based approaches decompose object space into a set of surfaces that in the following will be referred to as a *proxy geometry*. Graphics hardware primitives are usually planar. Thus the proxy geometry usually consists of polygons, albeit composite geometries like e. g. spherical shells [LMHJ99] [KW03] were proposed as well. In the latter case, the spherical shells are constructed using tesselation. In the more usual case using a planar proxy geometry, polygons are rendered in back-to-front or front-to-back order. The individual polygons constituting the proxy geometry are often referred to as *slices*. Two methods are prevalent: *object-aligned slices* used with 2D texturing and *viewport-aligned slices* used with 3D texturing.

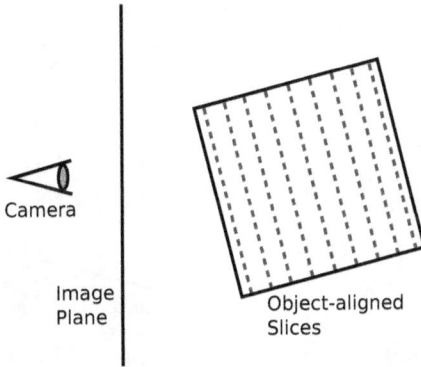

Figure 3.4: Object-aligned slicing. Slices are drawn parallel to the object axes of the volume dataset. Colors and transparency are assigned from 2D textures. Quadrangles can be precomputed and 2D texture lookup is more efficient than 3D texture lookup. On the downside, bilinear interpolation will result in a poor reconstruction of the 3D function inherent to the volume dataset.

Object-aligned slicing (cf. Figure 3.4) samples the volume datasets in object space using pre-calculated quadrangles. The quadrangles are drawn parallel to one of the object axes of the volume dataset. The volume dataset is organized into a set of 2D textures with one texture per quadrangle. The 2D textures provide colors and transparency values obtained e. g. by applying a transfer function (cf. Subsection 2.4.4). Then the quadrangles are rendered in back-to-front or front-to-back order while applying the appropriate compositing equation. The continuous function represented by the volume dataset is typically reconstructed using bilinear interpolation, which can be performed fast by modern graphics hardware. This approach has several disadvantages. 2D textures provide fast lookup using bilinear interpolation but will result in a poor reconstruction compared to e. g. trilinear interpolation using 3D textures. Another shortcoming of the object-aligned slicing approach are visual artifacts that become visible if the volume dataset is rotated so that the axis the slices are drawn along is almost perpendicular to the normal of the image plane. In that case, the volume dataset appears to have holes because one can see through the quadrangles used as proxy geometry. This shortcoming can be mitigated by having one stack of quadrangles and textures per object axis and flipping depending upon

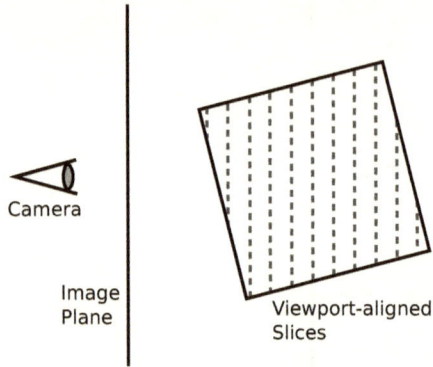

Figure 3.5: Viewport-aligned slicing. Slices parallel to the image plane are used to sample a 3D texture. Intersection polygons need to be recreated each time the virtual camera moves. 3D texturing enables trilinear or higher-order reconstruction kernels.

the angle between object coordinate axis and the normal to the image plane. While the hole artifacts can be hidden this way, each time the quadrangle stack gets flipped, the appearance of the image will change recognizably due to compositing accuracy and due to the fact that the direction in space of the bilinear interpolation operation changes. On top of that, the memory requirements triple with this approach.

The term *viewport-aligned slicing* is a bit misleading because it suggests that slices are actually quadrangles that are aligned to the four corners of the virtual viewport entity maintained by graphics application programming interfaces (APIs). In contrast to that, the technique referred to as viewport-aligned slicing assumes that object space is sampled using planes that are parallel to the image plane (cf. Figure 3.5). Because the term viewport-aligned slicing is used throughout the literature, this expression is adopted by this work, anyway.

With slices parallel to the image plane, the proxy geometry cannot be precomputed. In general the proxy geometry will also not consist of quadrangles only. The proxy geometry is created by sampling the volume using parallel planes with equal distances. For each plane the intersection with the bounding box of the volume dataset needs to be calculated, which result in either a triangle, a quadrangle, a pentagon or a hexagon.

Like in the object-aligned slicing case, alpha compositing can then be performed in back-to-front or front-to-back order. Texture coordinates are calculated for the vertices of the intersecting polygons which are used to lookup colors and transparency values from a 3D texture. The continuous function represented by the volume dataset can be reconstructed using trilinear interpolation which is implemented by the fixed function pipeline of modern graphics hardware. Higher-order reconstruction kernels like e. g. tricubic interpolation can also be applied using programmable graphics hardware. Reconstruction using 3D textures will typically be slower than sampling 2D textures, but will in general produce more faithful results.

In order to speed up the proxy geometry generation process, portions of the box-plane intersection calculations can be transferred to the GPU. Rezk Salama and Kolb [RSK05] proposed to perform the intersection test in a vertex program. They employed this optimization to load balance the fragment stage of the rendering pipeline and the vertex stage, with the latter potentially being starved on GPUs that in these days did not yet implement a unified shader architecture. In their case, six vertices need to be transferred to the GPU per box per plane. If the intersection test produces a polygon consisting of less vertices, identical vertices will be generated. Duplicate vertices will result in degenerate triangles which will not contribute to the fragment stage of the rasterization pipeline. Zellmann and Lang [ZL13] showed that the proxy geometry generation can be accelerated by distributing the box-plane intersection calculations among a vertex program and a geometry program. Fast box-plane intersection tests are crucial if the volume dataset is not only organized into one single bounding box, but into a hierarchy of bounding boxes like a uniform grid or an octree (cf. e. g. Section 16.5 from [SSC02]). Such hierarchies are used to implement acceleration techniques like empty-space skipping [LMK03].

3.2.2 Frequency Domain Volume Rendering

Frequency Domain Volume Rendering [TL93] (FDVR) works by applying a discrete Fourier transform to the volume dataset and exploiting the fact that in the frequency domain, according to the *Fourier slice-theorem*, the volume dataset can be reconstructed using a *single slice*. This effectively reduces the complexity of volume reconstruction from $O(n^3)$ in terms of the participating voxels to $O(n^2 log\ n)$ time. Although extensions and even ports to GPUs were proposed [VKG04] [JvRLHK04], the major shortcomings of this technique remain

Increased Memory Demand. Since the Fourier transform outputs complex numbers, in general the size of the volume dataset at least doubles. On top of that, while reconstruction in the spatial domain is usually sufficient using e. g. one byte per voxel, this is not the case with frequency domain reconstruction. Totsuka and Levoy [TL93] e. g. stated, that for effective FDVR, 16 bytes per voxel are necessary.

Lack of Depth Cues. When extracting a single slice from the volume, the volume rendering integral can only be evaluated in parts. Specifically, absorption of light emitted by volume particles, i. e. occlusion, cannot be accounted for. This shortcoming can be mitigated e. g. by deploying a local reflectance model, but remains a major insufficiency of the FDVR method.

Given these shortcomings, and the fact that the complexity of DVR in the spatial domain can be reduced using other means, FDVR in general is not compatible to spatial domain algorithms and is thus not in wide use.

3.2.3 Shear-Warp Volume Rendering

The shear-warp algorithm [LL94] combines properties of image-order algorithms and object order-algorithms. Shear-warp algorithms usually act on uniform grids which are treated as stacks of image slices. This analogy is valid, given e. g. that CT-scanners often actually output stacked image data. The class of algorithms is based on two transforms. A *shear* transform converts the slices of the volume to a coordinate system where all viewing rays are parallel and perpendicular to the slices (cf. Figure 3.6 a.)). For perspective projections, this shear operation also includes a scale (cf. Figure 3.6 b.)). Then, the transformed slices are combined using one of the compositing equations to form an *intermediate image*. The ensuing *warp* transforms the intermediate image to the final image. Algorithms can exploit

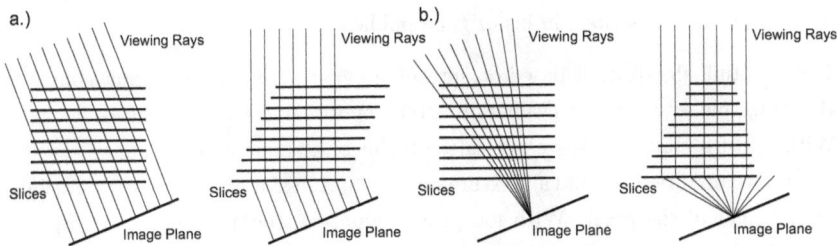

Figure 3.6: Shear factorization for the shear-warp algorithm. a.) converting the volume to sheared object space, where all parallel viewing rays are perpendicular to the volume slices, involves a shear transform. b.) In addition, for perspective projections, a scale transform of the volume slices is necessary. This figure was influenced by Figure 1 and Figure 2 from [LL94].

the property that voxels in *sheared object space* (i. e. after the shear transform was applied to the volume dataset) are aligned to pixels in the intermediate image. The shear-warp algorithm traditionally is targeted towards CPU implementations, where it can benefit from optimizations such as run-length encoding. This encoding scheme can typically be implemented more efficiently on CPUs than e. g. on GPUs, which are optimized for high throughput and rely on coherent memory accesses.

Schulze et al. [SNL01] elaborated on further optimizations to run the perspective shear-warp algorithm in virtual environments. Their optimizations comprised a reduced quality in order to guarantee constant frame rates. They identified the compositing step as the limiting factor and proposed to reduce its costs by combining fewer slices than present in the volume dataset, or by using intermediate images with a lower resolution than that of the actual display. In [SL02], the authors discussed parallelization issues of the perspective shear-warp algorithm for different HPC platforms.

3.2.4 Volume Splatting

Volume splatting is an object-order approach that was first proposed by Westover in 1989 [Wes89]. The ensuing description of the volume splatting algorithm is based on Westover's publication from 1990 [Wes90], which incorporates several enhancements to the algorithm described in his original publication.

The splatting algorithm is based on spreading *footprints* for each volume sample to the image plane. Footprint evaluation is the opposite operation to texture mapping. With texture mapping, the elliptical footprint of a single pixel in image space is mapped to texture space and all texture samples that the footprint overlaps contribute to the color of the pixel. With footprint evaluation, the contribution of a single volume sample is spread into image space, affecting every pixel the footprint overlaps.

Westover restricted himself to orthographic projection, which reduced footprint evaluation to only once per view computing the footprint as a template stored in a 2D lookup table and mapping this to image space using a constant 2D offset.

If the volume was equally spaced in all three dimensions of the uniform grid, the reconstruction kernel to determine the footprint from is a sphere, but in general, if the spacing of the grid differs among axes, the reconstruction kernel is an ellipsoid. The view-dependent footprint is then a *general* ellipse in screen space.

The screen space extent of the footprint to determine the dimensions of the lookup table is found by first transforming the unit sphere in matrix form U by the grid scale S, i. e. the real number in each dimension by which the grid has to be divided so that the spacing between grid cells equals one:

$$E = SU \tag{3.22}$$

Then the sample in *grid space* is transformed to screen space by applying the viewing transform V:

$$R = V^{-1T} E V^{-1} \tag{3.23}$$

The resulting matrix

$$R = \begin{pmatrix} A & D/2 & E/2 & 0 \\ D/2 & B & F/2 & 0 \\ E/2 & F/2 & C & 0 \\ 0 & 0 & 0 & -K \end{pmatrix} \tag{3.24}$$

can be interpreted as a general ellipsoid equation in quadric form:

$$K = Ax^2 + By^2 + Cz^2 + Dxy + Exz + Fyz \tag{3.25}$$

which can be solved for the x extent

$$x = \pm \sqrt{\frac{K}{A - \frac{D^2}{4B} - \frac{\left(E - \frac{DF}{2B}\right)^2}{4\left(C - \frac{F^2}{4B}\right)}}} \tag{3.26}$$

as well as for the y extent

$$y = \pm \sqrt{\frac{K}{B - \frac{D^2}{4A} - \frac{\left(F - \frac{DE}{2A}\right)^2}{4\left(C - \frac{E^2}{4A}\right)}}} \tag{3.27}$$

of the 2D footprint lookup table.

For mapping the projected ellipsoid to screen space, which results in a generally oriented ellipse, having the ellipsoid stored in quadric form is most useful. Then the screen space ellipse can easily be determined as

$$P = Xx^2 + Yy^2 + Zxy \tag{3.28}$$

with $X = \left(A - \frac{E^2}{4C}\right)$, $Y = \left(B - \frac{F^2}{4C}\right)$ and $Z = \left(D - \frac{EF}{2C}\right)$. The footprint can then be rendered by mapping points from the unit circle to the general ellipse.

While Westover's original algorithm from 1989 was restricted to MIP rendering, in his publication from 1990 he enhanced the splatting algorithm with full alpha compositing. To achieve this, he solved the sorting problem inherent to alpha compositing by using a so called *sheet buffer*. A sheet was a plane parallel to the image plane, which was swept in back-to-front or front-to-back order through the volume. For each sheet sampling position the intersecting volume samples were splatted to the sheet. The sheets themselves were then composited in the appropriate order, so that the correct overall traversal order was guaranteed. This approach is similar to the texture-based sampling using viewport-aligned slices described in Section 3.2.1.

There were many extensions to the original volume splatting algorithm. Laur and Hanrahan [LH91] proposed a hierarchical, progressive volume splatting approach. Mao et al. [MHK95] extended the algorithm to accommodate curvilinear grids. Their adjustment necessitated footprint recreation not only per view, but per view *and* per volume sample, so that a common footprint table was no longer applicable. Their slightly different footprint calculation method was fast enough to compute footprints on the fly. While Westover's original algorithm with one footprint table per view was only applicable to orthographic views where all footprints have the same extent regardless of their distance to the virtual camera, the footprint evaluation method from Mao et al. is also useful for volume splatting with a perspective view. Zwicker et al. [ZPvBG01] reduced aliasing artifacts using Gaussian resampling filters. Chen et al. [CRZP04] later presented a hardware-accelerated version of the same algorithm using GPUs.

Object-order approaches like volume splatting in general are useful because they not only allow for task parallelism but also for data parallelism. Volume samples can be handled almost independently and can thus be assigned to different processors which only need to communicate for compositing sheets. One of the problems that arise from volume splatting though is the relatively high sampling rate that is necessary to avoid annoying artifacts visible at the transitions between volume samples. On top of that, the sorting problem inherent to volume rendering can be solved more naturally using texture-based approaches or image-order approaches like ray casting, which is described in detail in Section 3.2.6.

3.2.5   Cell Projection

Most of the algorithms discussed so far are only applicable to regular grids. Arbitrary grid representations and especially unstructured grids demand for alternative algorithms that can cope with those grid types. The cell projection algorithm is capable of rendering *tetrahedra*. For regular grid types, which this thesis mainly focuses on, the algorithms described so far and in the remainder of this section may be a better match regarding performance. Cell projection, in contrast to e. g. ray casting (cf. Subsection 3.2.6), uses rasterization to output volumetric primitives to the screen.

Shirley and Tuchman [ST90] proposed a cell projection technique to display tetrahedra using graphics hardware and that can thus be used to render arbitrary unstructured grids, given that they have been *tetrahedralated* [She03], which is the analogous operation to triangulation in the 2D plane. The idea behind their projection algorithm was to render only outlines of the tetrahedra and send these as semi-transparent triangles to the graphics card. Decomposition of tetrahedra into triangles was view point dependent, so that one to four triangles were generated from the front facing boundaries of one tetrahedron for each change of the camera configuration. The opacity of a tetrahedron varied across the area of the triangles and depended on the thickness of the tetrahedron at the position of the projected image space fragment that the rasterizer evaluated. The thickness was accounted for by weighing the opacity by the Euclidian distance a hypothetical ray entering at this position would travel through the tetrahedron. To avoid having to perform ray integration at each fragment position, which was at that time not affordable with graphics hardware, ray integration was only performed at the thickest point of the tetrahedron and colors and opacity at the remaining positions were approximated using linear interpolation. Extinction was accounted for by applying the back-to-front compositing equation. When projecting tetrahedra, four basic projection types can occur that resulted in different sets of triangles to be rendered and that influenced the way the thickest point of the tetrahedron was determined.

Marroquim et al. [MMFE06] used two GPU passes to accelerate the cell projection algorithm. Their implementation used multiple render targets to project tetrahedra to image space in a first pass. *RGBA* textures were used to input data: one texture with 32 bits per channel that stored all vertices, another texture with 32 bits per channel that stored the four indices to vertices that formed the tetrahedra, and a third one with 8 bits per channel that stored the classification value. The shader executed during the first pass then projected the vertices to image space and tested for one of the four projection types. The output of the first shader program was stored to two 32 bit *RGBA* textures and contained the thickness of the tetrahedron, its centroid, the entry and exit intersection vertices that were determined based on the thickest point of the tetrahedron, as well as the number of the vertices needed to build up a triangle fan to rasterize this tetrahedron. The tetrahedra were then sorted in back-to-front order on the CPU, either based on an approximate bucket sort implementation used when the volume was animated or moving, or based on an $O(n \log n)$ sorting algorithm (merge sort) for still frames. Because sorting was performed based on the previously determined centroids of the tetradehedra, the authors mentioned that this approach is not guaranteed to produce "100% correct results in all cases". The second GPU pass then rendered the projected tetrahedra, with fragments corresponding to linearly interpolated tetrahedron vertex colors. The authors improved the image quality by applying partial pre-integration [MA04].

One shortcoming of the view point dependent cell projection approach is the fact that primitives must be drawn in back-to-front order. Although this is also true for the viewport-aligned, texture-based slicing approach (cf. Subsection 3.2.1), with the cell projection approach no implicit order is imposed upon the proxy geometry and thus back-to-front sorting is necessary. Alternative approaches [LCCK02] organized tetrahedra using space-partitioning data structures like octrees to sort them in an appropriate order or to apply level-of-detail to render data elements more coarse when they are further away from the viewer. Another shortcoming of rendering tetrahedra is the additional storage necessary when tetrahedralizing an arbitrary, unstructured grid.

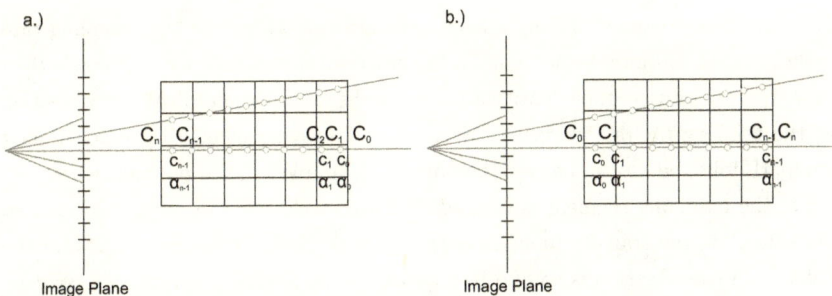

Figure 3.7: a.) Ray casting with back-to-front compositing. The image plane is sampled at pixel positions. Then, at each discrete sampling position along the ray, the value associated with the sample is determined using some interpolation scheme. After classification, the color values c_i are iteratively blended on top of the background intensity C_0 using the sampled transparency values α_i. C_n is the color that is output to the screen. b.) Ray casting with front-to-back compositing. If the product of the α_i reaches a threshold $1 - \epsilon$, ray traversal can be terminated early. C_n is the color that is blended with the background intensity and then eventually output to the screen.

3.2.6 Ray Casting

Ray casting [Lev88] is an image-order algorithm that solves the scattering equation by piecewise linear integration along the path of individual rays through the volume. Volume ray casting implementations are typically organized into one phase for primary ray setup and into another phase for integration and compositing. Primary rays integrate over image space, usually interpreting the set of image pixels as a uniform grid for regular or stratified sampling. Usually, at least one primary ray is assigned per image pixel. Then a single intersection with the bounding object of the volume is performed for each ray to decide whether to enter the integration phase or to assign the background color to the image pixel. The integration now depends on the characteristics of the volume density stored. The kinds of operations performed during integration depend on the type of the grid that is used. If the dataset is organized using a uniform grid, piecewise integration along the ray is typically implemented by using a ray marching approach. Each ray is traversed through the volume density in back-to-front- or front-to-back order (cf. Figure 3.7).

For that, a ray segment having a length that is proportional to the sampling rate is determined a priori. Depending on the traversal order, this ray segment is then moved through the volume density either from the exit position to the entry position of the primary ray or vice versa. Each time the ray segment is used to prolong the path followed along the ray, the volume is sampled at the position where the tip of the marching segment is located. With post-classification or pre-integrated classification, the transfer function is then sampled using this data value and the color from classification is composited on top of the already accumulated color by either using the back-to-front compositing equation or the front-to-back compositing equation. In the case of front-to-back compositing, ray traversal can be terminated early if the accumulated opacity reaches a certain threshold.

When the whole volume density was traversed, the accumulated color is stored in a data structure associated with the image pixel that the primary ray is assigned to. With supersampling, the color would than possibly be combined with other rendering results for that pixel, before finally being output to the screen for display or getting handed over to the visualization application for further post-processing.

3.2.7   Out-of-Core Volume Rendering

Out-of-core techniques are used when the volume dataset does not fit into the memory of the compute node which is used for rendering as a whole. This is often the case with GPU-accelerated volume rendering, where the amount of video memory is typically far lower than the amount of main memory available. In such cases, the volume dataset is subdivided into convex subobjects which fit into the video memory. If the underlying topology of the volume dataset is a uniform grid, these subobjects are usually axis-aligned boxes and the technique involved is called *bricking* [KMM+01] [RV06].

The bricks are then sent to the GPU for rendering sorted in back-to-front or front-to-back order, depending on the order used for alpha compositing. For reconstruction on the GPU, each brick is constructed with an appropriate amount of overlapping border voxels. The amount of additional voxels depends on the reconstruction filter used. Storing an excessive amount of border voxels increases the memory footprint of the rendering algorithm.

Bricking in general is applicable to all of the aforementioned DVR algorithms but is especially useful for the GPU-accelerated techniques. Bricking can also be useful in the context of cache access optimization (the technique is then referred to as *swizzling*, cf. Section 5.1.3) as well as for empty-space leaping accelerations. In the first case, brick sizes are chosen so that the content of an entire brick can fit into one cache line. In the latter case, whole bricks can be marked to contain the same value or even the zero value. Integration can then be simplified by striving over those regions with large steps while not having to actually enter the brick and load its whole content to memory at all.

Out-of-core rendering does of course not only have to be applied to the spatial extent of the volume dataset, but can be used e. g. to render large, time-dependent datasets. If the whole dataset does not fit into the memory of the GPU, but *a single* time step can be accommodated, out-of-core rendering can be thought of as a *streaming approach*, where only the content is streamed into memory that is needed at a certain instance in time.

3.3 Parallel Programming Models

In the course of the past decades, processor evolution coarsely followed *Moore's Law*, which predicts roughly a doubling of transistors per die every eighteen months. With die sizes shrinking considerably while retaining transistor count with every second generation of CPUs, since the past few years this evolution threatens to come to a halt. This is mainly due to lack of suitable manufacturing processes for ever smaller transistors, as well as due to the problem of heat dissipation that arises with such densely packed transistors. A strategy of the processor manufacturers to mitigate this hence is to increase the number of processor cores per package. Higher parallelism forces the software developer to be more aware of making her application *scale* to the increase in processor cores. *Amdahl's Law* [Amd67]:

$$S = \frac{1}{r_s + \frac{r_p}{n}} \tag{3.29}$$

provides a measure for the speedup S that is achievable with n processors, if the percentage of serial code r_s versus the percentage of parallelizable code r_p in a program is known. This relationship between speedup and the portion of code that is parallelizable makes it obvious how important it is to structure one's code to expose a large degree of parallelism, especially if n is growing, which generally can be assumed at least for the next few years.

Level of Parallelism	Programming Model
Instruction Level Parallelism	Mostly influenced by the compiler, programmer can help by avoiding pipeline stalls (e. g. exiting loops early). Today is less an issue because of shorter pipelines and sophisticated compiler architectures.
SIMD Instructions	Explicitly by using SIMD assembler instructions. Implicitly by using auto-vectorizing compilers. Programming languages like Fortran or Cilk Plus™ provide array notation that can be translated to vector instructions.
Multi-Core	Threading APIs like pthreads, Intel® Threading Building Blocks™ or OpenMP.
Local Area Network	Message Passing (MPI), explicit programming with sockets.
Accelerators	GPUs and the like. Can be used to offload entire parts of an algorithm. Typically expose a high degree of parallelism at the cost of an expensive context switch when transferring execution from the CPU to the coprocessor.

Table 3.1: Levels of parallelism exposed by HPC system and the typical means that the programmer can use to influence the behavior of her code.

HPC systems traditionally tend to be quite heterogeneous and thus expose parallelism on different levels. Table 3.1 provides an overview of the various levels and how they can be targeted by the programmer. The levels that need to be explicitly targeted by the programmer are covered in more detail in the remainder of this section.

Modern *processor cores* are typically built from small execution units like logic gates or *arithmetic logic units* (ALUs). Those execution units are often coupled using a pipeline approach [PH08], which is crucial to gain the high throughput achieved by modern processors. The length of the pipeline in the past often was the unique feature of the processor architecture. An increase in the pipeline depth reached its previous climax with the Netburst architecture incorporated into the Intel® Pentium 4™ [SGC01]. Since that release, architectures tended to expose a shorter pipeline in favor of an increase in CPU cores, which mitigated the pressure to keep an extremely deep pipeline filled with data items to be processed.

Each processor core of most modern CPUs has access to several general-purpose registers which usually store single fixed-point or floating-point items. In addition to that, they usually also possess *vector registers* and corresponding *vector instructions*, which act on the whole register while imposing a latency that is comparable to their corresponding general-purpose instruction. Section 3.3.1 goes into more detail regarding the programming models associated with this level of parallelism.

CPU architectures nowadays also tend to expose a higher degree of parallelism by having two or more CPU cores per CPU casing, yielding so called *multi-core* processors. HPC systems that accommodate several *CPU sockets* are referred to as *Symmetric Multiprocessing* (SMP) systems, because autonomous, yet usually identical CPU cores connect to a single shared memory. Section 3.3.2 introduces several SMP architectures as well as the programming models needed to optimize for this kind of system.

Distributed memory architectures mark the opposite end of the communication patterns introduced in this section. *Nodes* with local memory are connected using a fast interconnect like InfiniBand®. Though modern implementations provide means for fast memory exchange, communication patterns are typically prone to latency that is high compared to latency on SMPs. Section 3.3.3 introduces distributed memory architectures and the programming models associated with them.

More recent developments are based on enhancing the traditional compute system with an additional plug-in *accelerator* like a GPGPU. In the very beginning, GPUs implemented a fixed functionality that could not be adjusted by other means than configuration. With programmable shaders, these shortcomings were partially softened. Later, with unified shader architectures and even later with general-purpose programming APIs like NVIDIA® CUDA™, GPUs evolved into highly parallel processors which were optimized for extreme throughput and which could be used for arbitrary computations. Section 3.3.4 gives a general overview of modern GPGPU architectures and how they can be programmed. Section 3.3.5 introduces the x86-based Intel® Xeon Phi™ accelerator, which competes with GPGPUs since being deployed on a plug-in board that connects to the host processor over PCI Express and can be used to *offload* x86 code.

3.3.1 Single Instruction Multiple Data

The *Single Instruction Multiple Data* (SIMD) architecture is implemented by many modern CPUs, which provide additional registers for vector processing. The taxonomy that this term is based upon was introduced by Flynn in 1972 [Fly72], who distinguished parallel processors based on the way they process data elements. While multiprocessor systems typically execute a number of threads that operate on the same data items concurrently (see Section 3.3.2), SIMD execution units perform the same instruction on SIMD registers that can store multiple data items. The *SIMD width N* denotes the number of single-precision floating point data items that fit into one SIMD register. Modern CPUs exhibit SIMD widths ranging from 4 (e. g. SSE 4) to 16 (e. g. the upcoming AVX 512).

Instead of performing arithmetic operations on scalars, the operations are executed on a vector with essentially the same latency as their corresponding scalar instructions. SIMD instruction sets typically provide a mechanism to mask out data elements in the vector that do not participate in an operation. This allows the design of code paths with dynamic branches, without having to specify *jump* or *branch* instructions.

Rather than that, masks are used to decide whether a data element participates in an operation (*"if-branch"*), or if it doesn't (*"else-branch"*). Regarding these traits, it becomes immediately clear that masking in general is prohibitive. In the worst case, if there is only one data element left in the SIMD register to be processed, and the remaining data elements are inactive, the vector instruction essentially degrades to a simple scalar instruction.

Intrinsics are extensions to the programming language that some compilers provide. Modern compilers usually provide intrinsics to program the vector units of modern processors. Vector intrinsics spare the programmer from having to deal with a limited number of vector registers, register spilling or stack unwinding after function calls. Intrinsics provide low-level vector types that can accommodate basic integer or floating-point numbers and thus provide the programmer with strong type checking features normally known from high-level programming languages like C or C++. On the other hand, programming with vector intrinsics means being explicit about which specific vector instruction is called. Most modern compilers provide an *auto-vectorization* feature which generates vector instructions when called with appropriate optimization parameters. Anyway, in that case special care must be taken that the compiler is actually able to generate vector instructions for every single line of code. Context switches that occur when program execution transitions from vector registers to general-purpose registers or vice versa are prohibitive because they result in pipeline stalls on most modern CPUs.

Chapter 5 provides a detailed description of several SIMD implementations of the ray casting algorithm targeting various processor architectures. That chapter also goes into more detail on how vector intrinsics are used in the specific cases and on how code must be restructured to sufficiently benefit from the SIMD features of modern CPUs.

3.3.2 Shared Memory Computing

Traditional HPC *shared memory* systems accommodate multiple cores that are located in the housing of one node, that usually come with a shared chipset and that communicate with each other via a fast interconnect. This is opposed to distributed memory systems (cf. Subsection 3.3.3), where the compute cores are located on different nodes which communicate over a relatively slow, latency prone network interconnect. *Shared memory computing* (SMC) techniques exist that specifically map to the former. Different paradigms for Interprocess Communication (IPC) can be used, that are facilitated by modern operating systems [Ste98].

Native shared memory programming with the Unix operating system e. g. can be done by means of the POSIX Shared Memory API. This API provides ways for two processes to exchange data without having to copy it to a dedicated memory region. Instead of that, each process *maps* a region of the other process's memory. This is achieved by obtaining a pointer to a mapped memory region through the POSIX API. With the proper knowledge of what data is located in the mapped region, the process can then access the other process's data items without having to copy them to its own heap memory.

Multithreading APIs provide a more lightweight method of managing two parallel control flows that potentially access common memory items. In contrast to SMC with multiple processes, threads are required to be managed by a common parent process. This abandons the problem of having to keep track of the processes that mapped a shared memory region and only being able to destroy it if all processes released their handle to that region. Furthermore, threads tend to be a more lightweight entity on many operating systems regarding bookkeeping. With most multithreading APIs, accessing shared memory from two parallel control flows is quite natural, usually the control flow of a thread is executed through a callback function or a virtual member function, which can access the shared data via a pointer argument. This makes programming even simpler compared to mere shared memory programming, because the programmer does not have to care about the byte representation of the shared data items, but can access them using the native data structures used in the program. Multithreaded programming is facilitated by numerous operating system specific APIs like the POSIX Threads API (pthreads). In contrast to that, OpenMP [DM98] is a popular industry standard that many compiler vendors support and that facilitates multithreaded programming through annotation. This can be achieved by inserting preprocessor clauses and *pragmas* (which are hints to the compiler to perform a certain task in a specific way) into an ANSI C, ISO C++ or Fortran program which describes a serial control flow. Annotation-based parallelization is particularly popular because in theory, no changes to a serial code are necessary other than pragmas that are evaluated at compile time, thus retaining correctness given that the serial code was validated for correctness.

Shared memory systems are often distinguished based on locality properties of the memory that is attached to the cores. *Non-uniform memory access* (NUMA) systems [BSF+91] usually have local memory associated with each core, which is accessible from all the other cores. Some NUMA systems provide a global address space. Anyway, because of the memory locality, accessing memory that is located near the core imposes a lower latency than accessing memory that is far away. *Cache coherent non-uniform memory access* (ccNUMA) systems have a local, non-shared cache and a hardware abstraction layer that maintains cache coherence. While easier to program, ccNUMA chip design in general is more complex than ordinary NUMA chip design.

3.3.3 Distributed Memory Computing

A vast amount of textbooks is available that discuss the topic of distributed memory computing. The following considerations present only a very brief overview of the topic and are loosely based on the textbook by Peter Pacheco [Pac11]. *Distributed memory systems* (DMS) are comprised of multiple processors that are equipped with a local memory and which communicate via an interconnect that typically imposes high latency and limited bandwidth, especially when compared to the latency and bandwidth characteristics of SMPs. The more processors the DMS is comprised of, the more important grows the choice of topology of the underlying network interconnect. *Rings* or *tori* are typical cyclic network topologies found in DMS implementations. *Point-to-point* topologies become less simple to implement, the more processors are in use. *Hypercubes* can be a reasonable alternative to fully connected networks. There are several programming models available for programming DMSs. The most commonly available programming model is probably based on raw socket communication using the *internet protocol* (IP) in conjunction with the *transmission control protocol* (TCP) or the *user datagram protocol* (UDP). The two protocols, which basically differ in the guarantees that the protocol makes regarding the possible loss and the retrieval of data packages, are based on communication on several physical and logical layers. This stacked architecture naturally imposes latency only due to the use of a general-purpose protocol. Low-latency interconnects like InfiniBand® on the other hand can be programmed with non-standardized APIs provided by the manufacturer. A very popular standard that is in wide use by the HPC community and whose implementations use those low-level APIs is the *Message Passing Interface* (MPI). MPI does not rely on the TCP/IP stack, although it can be implemented on top of an IP-based network. The MPI programming model is essentially centered around processes that have a *rank* assigned with them. Processes typically, but not necessarily run on different processors. Processes are identified by their rank and roles like *master* or *slave* can be implemented based on them. Messages which are passed between processes may contain arbitrary data. In addition to point-to-point communication ("*unicast*"), broadcast communication is also possible.

3.3.4   General-Purpose Programming with NVIDIA® GPG-PUs

Graphics processing units (GPUs) in the previous decade developed from fixed-function, single-purpose coprocessors to most versatile multi-purpose data-parallel streaming processors (cf. Chapter 2 from [HKRS+06]). Shading languages allowed to freely program dedicated stages of the fixed-function pipeline [Ros09] like the vertex processing stage and the rasterization stage. At the same time, and in contrast to this graphics-oriented development, programming APIs emerged that allowed to freely program GPUs for general-purpose computations. What at first sounds like a contradiction at second thought turned out to be a viable approach. The development that turned GPUs from fixed-function processors into highly flexible compute nodes led to GPUs evolving into processors that can process a large amount of lightweight tasks simultaneously. As a consequence, researchers began to "abuse" the graphics APIs to port their high-throughput algorithms to GPUs. As a reaction to this development, general-purpose GPU APIs emerged that allowed to freely program GPUs using general-purpose languages like the C programming language.

Without having to worry about specifics related to graphics like using textures for storage or frame buffers to output results, porting scientific applications to GPUs highly improved the accessibility of this platform. The two most common *GPGPU* APIs today are NVIDIA® CUDA™ [SK10] and the open standard OpenCL [Khr13]. With their complex memory hierarchies, GPGPUs can be viewed as small NUMA systems that life on a plug-in card themselves. Contemporary GPGPUs expose an intricate memory hierarchy. A thorough understanding of that hierarchy is crucial to achieve efficient GPGPU implementations. The following description of the GPGPU programming model adapts the nomenclature that NVIDIA® uses in its hardware and API documentation [NVI13].

The system that contains the GPU and that provides the infrastructure to perform communication and memory copies to the GPU in the following will be referred to as the *host* or the *host system*, while the GPU itself will be referred to as the *device*. The same distinction will hold for the terms *host program* and *device program*, where the host program refers to the software program that initiates the execution of an algorithm on the GPU, e. g. by copying data to and from the GPU and providing control information.

Modern GPUs are organized into a set of *Streaming Multiprocessors* (SM). These correspond to the shader processors from the *unified shader architectures* [LNOM08] that modern GPUs are based upon. The SMs have a small on-chip *shared memory* attached to them that all threads scheduled on this SM can access with low latency. The DDR memory that is attached to the graphics board is referred to as *global memory*. Global memory can be accessed by all threads from all SMs, but for the price of lower bandwidth and higher latency. While the NVIDIA® CUDA™ documentation gives some insight into the latency involved with global memory accesses (i. e. 400 - 800 cycles depending on the compute capability of the GPU), it is less specific about the latency involved with shared memory access, stating that its latency is "much lower" than that of global memory.

The common programming model of NVIDIA® CUDA™ and OpenCL is based on an implicit SIMD approach. Groups of threads are scheduled by the SM in so called *warps*. E. g. on the NVIDIA Fermi™ [WKP11] architecture, a warp consists of 32 threads. No branch prediction is applied when the threads in the warp execute, i. e. if one thread enters a branch, all other threads will either execute the same branch or wait until the whole warp finished execution. NVIDIA® calls this approach *Single Instruction Multiple Thread* (SIMT). In contrast to the Intel® SIMD programming model, neither the SIMD width, nor masking of inactive SIMD lanes have to be accounted for, but are handled implicitly by the GPGPU API.

GPGPU *kernels* make up the device program and describe the control flow of a single thread in a warp. Kernels are typically programmed using structured programming languages. OpenCL programs can only be written using a subset of the ANSI-C programming language, while CUDA™ provides bindings for other languages like e. g. Fortran. Kernels are compiled into instructions for the specific GPU. The GPU code can either be generated at compile time of the host program or at run time, e. g. at program start or right before the algorithm will be executed on the device.

From within the device program, a memory hierarchy can be accessed, with the differing memory layers having different implications on latency and bandwidth of a memory access. *Global memory* can be read from and written to by every thread. With NVIDIA® devices manufactured before Fermi™, read accesses were not cached, which made them an expensive operation that needed to be minimized throughout the device program. With later architectures, global memory reads are cached. Global memory can directly be accessed from the host using memory copying instructions or direct memory access (DMA), on devices where this is supported. *Texture memory* is cached but read-only on the device and can be written to from the host. *Shared memory* can be accessed from all threads scheduled on the SM that the shared memory is attached to. Because warps are scheduled on one SM, shared memory accesses need to be synchronized explicitly. Accesses to global memory and texture memory are synchronized implicitly by the scheduler, who will wait for all SMs having executed the kernel before returning execution to the host program. Each thread also has access to a small amount of local registers.

GPGPU implementations can benefit from the massive parallelism provided by modern GPUs. Because of the weak branch prediction and the caching strategies that are less elaborate than the ones implemented on modern CPUs, GPU threads are a lightweight construct compared to CPU threads. GPUs are capable of hiding latency behind computation by providing massive parallelism. When programming GPGPU algorithms, it is often a good choice to avoid memory accesses by e. g. not storing pre-calculated results, but rather by computing these anew if needed. One major bottleneck of GPGPU algorithms nowadays is the communication overhead for copying data over PCI Express (PCIe), which is used by today's hardware to connect host and device. GPGPU algorithms at least need to amortize this overhead by exposing a sufficient amount of parallelism. Image-order DVR algorithms lend themselves well to GPGPU implementations, because threads can execute mostly in parallel if they are e. g. assigned to process one image pixel (cf. Section 3.4.2).

3.3.5 Programming Models for the Intel® Xeon Phi™ Co-processor

The Intel® Xeon Phi™ coprocessor is an x86-compatible accelerator that is attached to the host using PCI Express. A thorough overview of the underlying *Many Integrated Core* (MIC) architecture, formerly known as the *Knights Corner* architecture, can be found in [JR13]. In essence, the coprocessor is an SMP on a single chip, that is comprised of 50 or more cores and wide 512 bit SIMD units. The coprocessor that the author of this thesis has access to comes with 60 in-order cores that can run four concurrent hardware threads each. At its current state, the 60 in-order cores are connected using a bidirectional ring bus and each core is equipped with an 8-way 512 KB L2 cache. Each core is additionally equipped with an L2 *translation lookaside buffer* (TLB) that caches translations of virtual memory addresses to physical memory addresses, which evidently occur often on systems with many cores accessing a shared memory. An 8 GB GDDR5 RAM is accessible via the on-chip memory controller. The current version of the coprocessor comes with a dedicated 64 bit instruction set that is not backward compatible to its CPU counterparts but that offers some special commands like scatter / gather operations and hardware math instructions like fast reciprocal, power, exponential and square root functions.

The coprocessor can be viewed as a separate node which actually comes with full TCP- and InfiniBand® stacks, runs a Linux operating system and can be accessed using a secure shell. Following this design philosophy, Intel® thus proposes two execution modes for user-mode programs. *Native applications* run completely on the coprocessor. The user compiles her application in a way that the main routine of the program is assembled to the instruction set of the coprocessor. Then she copies the executable and all external libraries (which of course were also compiled for the coprocessor) to the Xeon Phi™ and connects to it e. g. using secure shell to execute the application. In contrast to that, *offload applications* are initiated on the host. Code portions that run on the coprocessor are separated into dedicated object files by the compiler. When the application is executed, the object code is handed over to the coprocessor using an operating system service running on the host. At the time of writing, object code for the Xeon Phi™ can only be created with the Intel® compiler suite.

Intel® advertises its accelerator to generally support each of the parallel programming models that are used to program ordinary SMPs. The Xeon Phi™ thus comes with support for the threading models described above, such as Posix Threads or OpenMP, as well as with an optimized MPI implementation. Key to scaling to the MIC architecture, in addition to exploiting thread parallelism, is vectorization to exploit the 512 bit SIMD registers. These can e. g. be programmed by using auto-vectorization. A more explicit means is the Intel® Cilk Plus™ programming language [Int14], which provides an array notation which is similar to that of the Fortran programming language and which can be used to formulate an algorithm in terms of vector operations. An even more explicit means is to directly use the vector instructions of the MIC architecture, e. g. by using MIC vector intrinsics which act on 512 bit fixed- or floating-point built-in data types that internally map to the 32 available SIMD registers.

For graphics applications, the preferred mode of operation is most likely offloading. Although in fact a native application model is at least imaginable - e. g. by using the VNC protocol [RSFWH98] or X server forwarding - additional overhead due to network traffic and having to perform unoptimized rendering in software would be unreasonably high with this execution model. Intel® proposes two programming models for offloading to the coprocessor. One programming model is based on annotations. The portions of the code that shall be offloaded are marked using preprocessor *pragma* clauses. Data can be send to and from the coprocessor by specifically marking it as *in, out* or *inout* data, which is then either copied to the device prior to the computation, copied back to the host after computation, or both. Allocation is handled in a similar manner using pragma directives. An alternative approach to offloading is exposed through the Cilk Plus™ programming language. Cilk Plus™ is based on a shared memory approach. Cilk Plus™ essentially is an extension to the C/C++ programming language, which adds several language constructs for parallel programming. One of these language constructs enables to call an offload function or execute an offload code block on the coprocessor. With Cilk Plus™ nevertheless, data is shared among host and device using a common address space rather than being copied explicitly.

3.4 Parallel Direct Volume Rendering Techniques

This section starts with a classification of parallel rendering algorithms in general. Different architectures lend themselves more or less well to algorithms being categorized based on this classification. GPGPU ray casting on one GPU e. g. is a candidate for an image space parallelization, while object space parallelization is applicable to distributed rendering scenarios on Multi-GPU systems or on distributed memory systems. Load balancing issues are addressed in the remainder of the section. This section will only provide a theoretical background of the parallelization techniques. A more thorough investigation based on actual implementations as well as results from performance measurements can be found in Chapter 5.

3.4.1 Sorting Classification for Parallel Rendering

The sorting classification for parallel rendering proposed by Molnar et al. [MCEF94] was widely adopted by the high performance graphics community. The authors argued that assigning post-processed data (i. e. data that was prepared for rendering, such as geometry from surface rendering or proxy geometry for volume data) and pixels to processors can be viewed as a sorting problem. The main stages involved in rendering and finally displaying an image are the geometry processing stage and the rasterization stage. At the geometry stage, 3D primitives are processed and finally converted to *fragments* in image space. At the rasterization stage, the fragments are processed to obtain the final color for the respective image pixels. Workload assignment is then a sorting problem regarding the order in which the results generated by the participating processors contribute to the final image. Based on this proposition, the authors distinguished three classes of parallel rendering algorithms that depended on the stage in the rendering pipeline where the sorting happens.

With *sort-first* parallel rendering, sorting is performed most early in the rendering pipeline. Image space is initially divided into a set of disjoint regions that cover the whole 3D viewport occupied by the application. Often a tiled subdivision is used. Image tiles are then assigned to processors. The tiles are then rendered in parallel and are finally stored to their respective region in a shared frame buffer or the local frame buffer of one or more dedicated processors which are responsible for image construction. The granularity of the subdivision into tiles can be exploited for load balancing. The tiles can e. g. be served to the processors on demand from a priority queue whenever a processor is starved. Image space subdivision can also be performed hierarchically e. g. using *quadtrees* (cf. e. g. Section 16.5 from [SSC02]) to circumvent the shortcomings of a high granularity and having to manage a large queue with many tiles, without risking to starve some of the rasterization processors for a significant amount of time.

With the *sort-middle* approach, post processed data as well as pixels are distributed among the processors. Sorting happens in-between the geometry stage and the rasterization stage. Some processors in the pipeline are assigned post processed data, while other processors are assigned regions of image space. Data that was processed in parallel on the geometry stage is then passed on to the rasterization stage. The rasterization stage processes *fragments* in parallel. The data flow from the geometry stage to the rasterization stage usually contains geometry in the form of fragments that were transformed to image space e. g. by applying perspective projection, frustum culling and clipping. While the sort-middle approach is usually found in graphics hardware, the parallel visualization pipelines of common visualization software are realized using either sort-first or sort-last parallel rendering.

Sort-last parallel rendering performs the sort after the rasterization stage. Geometry processing and rasterization are performed by the participating processors in parallel, resulting in one *intermediate image* per processor. These independently rendered images are eventually assembled to a final image using compositing. In the presence of transparency, alpha compositing is applied, while with opaque geometry that was rendered to a z-buffer, depth compositing is applied where only the frontmost fragment from all intermediate images contributes to the final image.

Sort-last rendering has the advantage over sort-first rendering that it accomplishes data parallelism by design. This can be an important factor for DVR, where the size of the volume datasets grows with the third power of their spatial resolution. Sort-first approaches do not naturally lend themselves well to data parallelism, because in general it cannot be predetermined which parts of the post processed data will occupy a certain region in image space for an arbitrary camera transformation. DeMarle et al. [DGBP05] and later Ize et al. [IBH11] proposed to circumvent this shortcoming by using a caching strategy called *Distributed Shared Memory* (DSM). Sort-first rendering on the other hand can benefit from frame-to-frame coherence and load balancing that is more easily applicable. Sort-middle rendering algorithms are hard to scale to systems with large amounts of processors because image pixels and geometry need to be reassigned to processors per frame, which results in a tremendous amount of time spent for communication overhead.

3.4.2   Sort-First Volume Ray Casting

The ray casting algorithm is especially well suited for a sort-first parallel GPGPU implementation on NVIDIA® CUDA™ GPUs. In that case, GPU kernels are implemented so that one GPU program assigned to a single thread implements the complete ray marching procedure for exactly one ray. The GPGPU implementation can benefit from the trilinear interpolation capabilities that the GPUs implement efficiently when sampling the volume dataset at discrete positions. With the CUDA™ programming model, multiple threads will be scheduled in a warp. Nevertheless, the restrictions to branching of threads in a warp will only result in slight efficiency drops because of the coherent traversal scheme of the ray marching procedure. Neighboring rays will exit the volume at nearby positions and on top of that are likely to access the same volume elements, resulting in an efficient utilization of the caches that are attached to global memory and to texture memory. For the NVIDIA® Fermi™ architecture [WKP11] and later architectures, NVIDIA® significantly improved the scheduler that launches warps on Streaming Multiprocessors. Implementations targeting NVIDIA® GPUs from prior generations will benefit from a *persistent thread* scheduling approach as it is e. g. described in [AL09] or [GSO12]. With a persistent thread approach, image space is subdivided into regions with sizes aligned to the warp size of the GPU. On each Streaming Multiprocessor, one warp of threads is started that is persistent throughout the rendering process for one image and immediately acquires a region to render. When a warp finishes rendering a region, a dedicated thread from the warp increments a counter in shared memory and the whole warp processes the next region until there are no more regions left. Incrementing the shared memory counter can efficiently be performed using atomic operations. Persistent thread approaches resemble the general task queue approaches [CT08]. Chen et al. [CVKG10] raise the approach to actually have the CUDA™ kernels persistent, which are then served new work from the CPU.

GPGPU ray casting can efficiently be parallelized for Multi-GPU systems using sort-first rendering (cf. Section 3.4.4) as well as sort-last rendering (cf. Section 3.4.3). For DVR with mere local illumination, the communication overhead imposed on the ray marching algorithm by either approach is minimal, so that the overall overhead for sending data over the PCIe interface is negligible. Nevertheless, certain modalities like large volume datasets or in situ visualization scenarios [Ma09] can make it a viable option to perform volume rendering on the CPU. Knoll et al. [KTW+11] present a SIMD CPU volume ray casting implementation for large volume datasets. CPU ray casting implementations typically cannot compete with GPU implementations in terms of interactivity due to their lack of 3D texture support in hardware and because they currently do not expose as high a level of parallelism as GPUs do. Nevertheless, as will be shown in this thesis, with sophisticated implementations, DVR on CPUs is at least on the verge to being computed interactively with frame rates of 30 Hz or higher. CPU implementations like the one proposed by Knoll et al. or the one proposed in Chapter 5 can even be superior to GPGPU implementations. Specifically, when rendering very large datasets, one may benefit from the more sophisticated cache organization of modern CPUs. CPU memory nowadays is also usually larger than GPU memory by at least an order of magnitude, so that larger datasets can be accommodated without having to use out-of-core techniques like the ones described in Section 3.2.7. Chapter 5 describes a parallel rendering system, where a Multi-GPU system using CUDA^{TM} GPGPU ray casting is accompanied by a CPU SIMD ray casting implementation.

3.4.3 Sort-Last Parallelization for Multi-GPU Systems and Distributed Memory Systems

Sort-first parallel DVR and GPGPU systems are a powerful combination because the SMs are all attached to memory that can be accessed with relatively low latency. In situations where memory is local to the participating processors, and interprocess communication incurs a high overhead, sort-last parallelization can be the method of choice. Communication that involves the interconnect of the mainboard, main memory, or even a network interconnect between nodes of an HPC system typically incurs such an overhead.

A rather new development is the use of more than one GPU per node to perform rendering. Marchesin et al. [MMD08] proved the general feasibility of Multi-GPU systems for DVR. They analyzed Multi-GPU DVR with texture-based and ray casting-based implementations and report almost linear scalability, e. g. a speedup of 3.5 using 4 GPUs for a small dataset. With datasets that did not fit into the texture memory of a single GPU, and that needed to be rendered using out-of-core methods before, they even reported speedups of factor 8, which is due to the decrease in communication between mainboard and GPUs for rendering. Their findings prove that Multi-GPU systems are a hardware platform that is extremely viable for DVR and specifically for large datasets.

Volume datasets of the form (X, S, T), $X \in \mathbb{N}^3$, $S \in \mathbb{R}$ and $T \in \mathbb{N}$ (i. e. uniform grids and scalar data) are especially simple to parallelize using sort-last because uniform grids can easily be subdivided into convex objects: subdividing once along an axis-aligned plane at an arbitrary inner border between cells yields a subdivision into two new uniform grids. Although a uniform subdivision may suffice for certain cases, higher scalability can be achieved by using hierarchical space subdivision schemes.

A popular space subdivision scheme in computer graphics is one that splits objects along all of their principal axes using a hyperplane in a *divide and conquer* manner. In two dimensions, this yields a so called *quadtree*, while its three-dimensional counterpart is called an *octree* [SSC02]. A general space subdivision scheme is the k-d tree [Ben75]. k-d trees are also created using a *divide and conquer* approach. The subdivision starts by assigning the axis-aligned bounding box (AABB) of the uniform grid to the root of the k-d tree. Each tree node is then further split based upon some heuristic. The split is performed by finding the most appropriate principal axis based on that heuristic and by then determining the most appropriate position to locate a hyperplane (which is an actual plane in three dimensions) that splits the AABB of the node into two halves. Each half becomes a new node. The heuristic is also used to terminate the subdivision. The k-d tree is a special case of the general family of *BSP trees*. The two of them differ in that for k-d tree creation, an axis-aligned subdivision is performed, while BSP trees are created using arbitrary split planes. This extra flexibility is typically not needed when hierarchically organizing volume data that was sampled on a uniform grid.

After finding an appropriate subdivision, the leaf nodes of the space partitioning data structure are assigned to one rendering processor each. Each processor can then perform rendering without even knowing that it is only responsible for a partial dataset. Care has only to be taken about an overlap at the inner borders of the subvolumes. These may be necessary to perform correct (e. g. trilinear) interpolation at the borders or for correct gradient estimation for local illumination (cf. Section 3.1). The image that each processor creates only depicts a subset of the volume dataset and must contain an alpha channel. Using the k-d tree, sorting these *intermediate images* is then particularly easy by performing an *in or out* test with the current camera position and the two half-spaces at each level of the tree and visiting the "back" node first.

The intermediate images are then assembled to form the final image using alpha compositing, which involves communicating image data between processors. In its most simple variant, compositing is not parallelized but performed by each rendering processor sending its *complete* intermediate image to the processor that is responsible for display. Sort-last image compositing per se is a *reduction* problem, because a parallel summation over a set of distributed data items needs to be computed. In the special case of *alpha* compositing, that summation is not associative and the summand's contributions are weighed according to their order. With many rendering processors, it can easily become the bottleneck restricting the performance of sort-last parallel rendering algorithms. In order to reduce bandwidth pressure on the interconnect used, several optimizations were proposed in the literature to parallelize that task.

Direct send compositing [Neu94] [EP07] works as follows. In addition to the data partitioning, screen space is partitioned into n disjoint tiles. This partitioning can be arbitrarily chosen e. g. for best pixel read-back performance. After each processor has performed rendering, it performs pixel read-back for the $n - 1$ tiles it is not responsible for and sends each of them to its $n - 1$ counterparts. In consequence, each processor receives $n - 1$ tiles. Each processor then performs alpha compositing for the tile it is responsible for, e. g. by using a GPU. In many cases, a distributed result may be acceptable. In cases where this is not desired, the $n - 1$ processors read back the tile they are responsible for and send it to the processor responsible for display (given that one of the n rendering processors is responsible for rendering *and* display).

Direct send compositing can lead to network contention due to many simultaneous messages [BCH12]. Tree-based compositing algorithms like *binary swap* [lMPH94] can help to mitigate this pressure by applying a subdivision based on *divide and conquer*. The compositing algorithm achieves this by adjusting the size of the communicated image based on the locality of the communication. The algorithm works as follows: n processors may participate in the compositing algorithm, where $n = 2^m$ and $m \in \mathbb{N}$ (i. e. n is a *"power of two"*). The algorithm is performed in multiple *rounds*. After having rendered their intermediate image, each *two* neighboring processors *swap* the opposite half of their composited image. The recipient unites its incoming half with

the image that it retrieved so far by applying a compositing operator. With each
round, the image portion that is swapped between processors is divided by half, while
locality decreases. During the second round, each two processors swap a quarter
of their already assembled image, but with their second to nearest neighbor. This
procedure of halving the image size and doubling the distance between processors
continues until the size of the swapped image portions equals $\frac{1}{n}$ of the original image
size. The relation between message size and communication distance allows for an
increased scalability compared to direct send.

One major shortcoming of binary swap compositing is, that it is only applicable
for a *power of two* processor count. This is due to the fact that the size of each
communication group is limited to two. The 2-3 Swap algorithm [YWM08] adapts
the Binary Swap algorithm to cope with arbitrary processor counts. This is achieved
by exploiting the observation that any integer greater than one can be represented
through a sum of twos and threes. Initially, a *compositing tree* with k levels is
constructed recursively. From that, the group sizes and communication patterns of
tree-based algorithms can be deduced. Tree construction works as follows. For an
arbitrary $N \in \mathbb{N}$, N being the number of processors participating in compositing,
let $K \in \mathbb{N}$ and $2^{K-1} \leq N < 2^K$. Then the compositing tree is constructed by
successively assigning the processor count n of the current round and partitioning it
into two sets L and R, so that $l = |L| = \lfloor \frac{n}{2} \rfloor$ and $r = |R| = \lceil \frac{n}{2} \rceil$. Further, let $d = K$
initially. For each round, if $r < 2^d$, create two child nodes, otherwise create three
child nodes from a new partitioning L, M and R, $l = |L| = \lfloor \frac{n}{3} \rfloor$, $m = |M| = \lfloor \frac{n}{3} \rfloor$
and $r = |R| = \lceil \frac{n}{3} \rceil$. Then proceed by recursively repeating this procedure for each
child and adjusting n and d to the current round. Note that for N being a power
of two, the resulting compositing tree will correspond to that from binary swap.
Otherwise, the compositing tree obtained by this procedure will reduce variation in
group sizes and thus the complexity imposed by the compositing algorithm. During
image compositing, after each round groups are merged together and image portions
are exchanged, just as this is the case with binary swap. Because groups may either
be of size two or three, maintaining the order is slightly more complicated and is
obtained by using a procedure that takes the processor count per group at the next
level in the tree into account.

While the group sizes k_i, with i being an index over the number of communication groups per round r in 2-3 swap were limited to two or three, the radix-k algorithm [PGR+09] generalizes compositing by allowing more combinations of $k = (k_1, k_2, ..., k_r)$ and r. All groups in one round have the same size and direct send compositing is performed in each communication group. Within each round, any factorization $\prod_{i=1}^{r} k_i = N$ is permitted. This makes direct send as well as binary swap special cases of the radix-k algorithms.

Bethel et al. [BCH12] report timing results for the four sort-last compositing algorithms and conclude that the radix-k algorithm is not only more flexible than traditional approaches like direct send or binary swap, but can even outperform them by several factors.

Because of the huge amount of samples that need to be accumulated during integration, DVR in general is highly susceptible to asymptotic errors [EJR+13] due to the finite accuracy of floating-point computations [Gol91]. This can become especially displeasing in the context of sort-last parallel rendering. In that case, round-off errors accumulate independently among the processors, which can cause artifacts at the transitions between the subvolumes [BPT02]. Strategies to mitigate this effect include rendering using higher computational accuracy or rendering using more rendering contexts than there are processors. In the latter case, smaller subvolumes can be rendered, which naturally require less samples and thus reduce the likelihood of tremendous errors. Both strategies induce increased overhead that can influence the overall performance of the compositing calculations.

3.4.4   Load-Balancing for Parallel Direct Volume Rendering

Parallelization of the DVR algorithms can typically result in load imbalances. With sort-last, if two processors take part in rendering and the volume is equally shared between them, load imbalances can occur if one processor renders its part faster than the other processor. In that case, load imbalances can stem from multiple sources. If the two processors in general have different capabilities and these capabilities can be *quantified*, *load-balancing*, i. e. the distribution of work as a reaction to load imbalances, is easily achieved. If load imbalances stem from factors like camera orientation or a dynamically adjustable transfer function, load-balancing with sort-last is in general not easily achievable because it would typically imply transferring whole volume chunks from one processor to the other.

Nevertheless, load imbalances are even more imminent with sort-first parallel algorithms because they are largely influenced by dynamic camera adjustments and must thus be accounted for each frame anew. Sort-first load-balancing schemes are often task queue based, like the persistent thread approach that is e. g. used by the GPGPU implementation described in Chapter 5. Here the work is subdivided into tasks by splitting screen space into tiles. Threads are generated persistently at the beginning of the program execution and idle while no work needs to be done. When the task queue is filled with new screen space tiles, the threads become busy until the task queue is empty again. That way, threads can be kept persistent and no thread creation overhead is necessary for each frame. On top of that, the workload is balanced because threads do not idle as long as there is work left in the queue.

A persistent thread approach is often accompanied by organizing screen space tiles along a space-filling curve [KA97]. That way, locality can be exploited. If one processor acts upon a specific region of screen space, with coherent datasets it is likely that the data items that are currently in memory or even in the cache of the processor can be reused for the work that is associated with the neighboring tile.

Cosenza et al. [CDE13] based *dynamic load-balancing* for sort-first surface ray tracing on a cost estimate that was computed on the GPU and stored in a G-buffer. This was then used for load-balancing by assigning costs to screen space tiles, which were split based on the cost estimate and then enqueued to the task queue for rendering. That way, tiles with a high workload could be rendered first, which was beneficial because when rendered first, the workload could effectively be hidden.

3.5 Direct Volume Rendering and Visualization Systems

This section reviews visualization systems that incorporate Direct Volume Rendering. Along with a discussion of which specific algorithms are used by the respective visualization system, a brief review is provided of how Direct Volume Rendering is integrated into the overall execution model of each system. Each of the discussed visualization systems is either open source, or the source code of the visualization system is available to the author of this thesis for inspection.

3.5.1 ImageVis3D

ImageVis3D [FK10] is a mere DVR application with cross-platform support and whose user interface is based on Qt [Qt 14]. ImageVis3D includes the *Tuvok* subsystem as a DVR library. Tuvok implements a variety of DVR algorithms, ranging from 2D and 3D texture-based volume rendering to shader-based GPU ray casting. Tuvok uses OpenGL® as well as DirectX® as underlying low-level graphics APIs, depending on the platform it was compiled for. Large datasets can be accommodated by using out-of-core rendering techniques (cf. Section 3.2.7). Progressive rendering allows for interactive frame rates by adapting the quality of the images to the desired frame rate, making use of level of detail (LOD) techniques. The ImageVis3D graphical user interface (GUI) as well as the Tuvok DVR library can be extended using plugin mechanisms provided by the respective APIs. An ImageVis3D implementation exists that brings DVR to the iOS operating system. This implementation actually runs on the client tablet or phone and is based on OpenGL® for Embedded Systems (OpenGL® ES™).

3.5.2 Voreen

Voreen [MSRMH09] is a visualization system that is centered around DVR. Voreen is based on a dataflow network approach where *processors* represent the network nodes and are used to implement DVR algorithms or auxiliary structures like clipping planes. Voreen's DVR algorithms are implemented using OpenGL® . In addition to mere volume rendering, Voreen supports annotation of volumes using labels, glyph rendering, speedlines to visualize motion, and various additional features. With its dataflow network approach, Voreen allows for rapid-prototyping. Voreen comes with several GLSL-based ray casting implementations, that support either isosurface rendering, MIP (cf. Section 3.1) or DVR, which can be chosen from using run time compilation.

3.5.3   DeskVOX

DeskVOX [Des14], which abbreviates "VOlume eXplorer for the Desktop", is a mere DVR application. The Virvo DVR library [SWWL01] is at the heart of the application and implements the DVR algorithms. The Virvo library mainly supports volume datasets that are defined on uniform grids. Virvo provides implementations of the various types of DVR algorithms (see Section 3.2): a Shear-Warp Volume Rendering implementation as well as a CPU ray casting implementation using SSE 4.1 for running on Intel® x86- and Intel® x86-64-compatible CPUs, texture-based DVR using either 2D textures, stacked 2D textures or 3D textures, a ray casting implementation targeting the Intel® Xeon Phi™and a GPGPU ray casting implementation based on NVIDIA® CUDA™. Most of the algorithms implemented in Virvo perform post-classification. Shaders for transfer function lookup are provided that support various dimensionalities that the data items at the voxels may have.

DeskVOX itself is an application with a lightweight user interface based on Qt. The UI provides means to edit 1D- and 2D transfer functions, with the rendered image adapting to the changes in real-time, as well as several other interaction means with the volume data, such as editable regions of interest or clipping planes, that can be used to create partial views of the volume dataset. DeskVOX comes with utilities to convert general data files storing structured volume data to the native format interpreted by the Virvo library.

During the course of writing this thesis, several DVR algorithms or related methods were integrated into the Virvo library, so that DeskVOX now also possesses facilities e. g. for parallel DVR (cf. Chapter 5) on several hardware platforms, and image-based remote rendering. Because the COVISE visualization software (see Section 3.5.6) also uses the Virvo library to perform DVR, most of the features available in DeskVOX are accessible from COVISE too.

3.5.4 ParaView

Unlike ImageVis3D, Voreen and DeskVOX, which are visualization systems that are centered around DVR, ParaView [Kit14a] [Hen04] (as well as each of the visualization systems summarized in the remainder of this section) is a full-fledged visualization system that integrates DVR as a component of a wide variety of visualization algorithms. ParaView is based on a demand-driven dataflow network [Mor09]. Demand driven dataflow networks function in a bottom-up fashion, i. e. nodes that are chronologically located at the end of the acyclic dataflow graph and are typically *sinks* like renderers, send messages to the *source* nodes at the beginning and demand that they make data available.

ParaView is based on the *Visualization Toolkit* (VTK) [Kit14b] [SML06], which is used to implement a vast variety of visualization algorithms. Among those algorithms are also facilities to perform DVR. Anyway, VTK does not support parallel DVR algorithms of large datasets.

3.5.5 VisIt

VisIt [Vis14] [ABW+13] [CBB+05] is a general visualization system that is in wide use in several scientific communities like meteorology or natural sciences in general. Unlike ParaView or COVISE, VisIt does not support to visually program the visualization pipeline using a dataflow network, but provides the visualization algorithms through disconnected modules. VisIt is based on a client-server architecture and specifically provides remote rendering facilities. VisIt comes with several hardware accelerated and software DVR algorithms, namely splatting, texture-based rendering and ray casting. Although targeted towards large scientific datasets, VisIt currently offers no support for large volume datasets and thus relies on downsampling before being able to display the dataset.

3.5.6   COVISE

COVISE [RLL$^+$96] is a visualization software that is based on an event-driven dataflow network, i. e. on execution of the network, data is distributed to the modules in a top-down fashion. COVISE facilitates the interactive post-processing phase by providing modules that can interface with simulations or that can read simulation results from file systems. Algorithms like cutting surface calculation or particle tracing (cf. Section 2.4) can be used to process the data for rendering. COVISE provides several grid data types, that can be displayed using renderer modules. Different renderer modules exist, an Open Inventor-based [Wer93] renderer is used for desktop environments, while the renderer COVER is used for Virtual Reality applications. COVER comes with a 3D GUI that can be used to interact with virtual environments.

For Direct Volume Rendering of structured grids, COVISE uses the Virvo library, which is also used for DVR in DeskVOX (see Section 3.5.3). Virvo integrates with COVISE in several ways. COVISE itself provides modules to read and write volume datasets to and from the file system. In addition to that, the structured grid COVISE data type can be converted to Virvo *volume descriptions*, which hold the packed volume data along with additional meta information. Because of the various algorithms that are provided by COVISE, volumes need to be rendered in conjunction with opaque geometry. The DVR algorithms themselves are integrated into COVISE as a plugin for the desktop renderer and the VR renderer. While the desktop renderer only provides facilities for mere viewing of the volumes, the VR renderer COVER has an advanced GUI with a transfer function editor that can be used in virtual environments. Through the integration of the algorithms described in this thesis into the Virvo library (cf. Section 5.3), advanced features like parallel DVR on Multi-GPU systems and distributed memory systems are freely available in COVISE and COVER.

Chapter 4

A Software Architecture for Distributed Volume Rendering

The implementation of a DVR software designed to run on HPC systems requires a heterogeneous and flexible software architecture. Not only must the system provide parallel rendering facilities, but also support for the specific types of hardware that the actual rendering is performed on, support for different kinds of network interconnect, as well as multi-user support. The following section recommends an architecture for such a DVR software based on a pipeline approach. These recommendations and results were published by Zellmann and Lang [ZL12]. This section is heavily based upon the research from this paper. Figures 4.1 through 4.3 were originally published as part of the paper and are reprinted with friendly permission of IASTED.

An implementation based on the software architecture proposed in the remainder of this section was integrated into the DVR library Virvo (cf. e. g. [Sch03]). Where this is helpful, the theoretical descriptions of the underlying concepts of the software architecture are accompanied by a description of implementation details that illustrate why certain design decisions were made.

4.1 Distributed Volume Rendering

In contrast to mere parallel DVR, with rendering systems running on HPC systems a broader definition for DVR using parallel resources in a multi-user context is necessary. In order to derive a working definition, the term *Distributed Volume Rendering* unites all varieties of volume rendering on parallel hardware. Parallelization on HPC systems cannot be solely applied in terms of the sorting classification described by Molnar et al. [MCEF94]. Datasets consisting of multiple time steps can be distributed so that the time steps are processed in parallel. If more than one user accesses the HPC system to perform volume rendering, distribution of parallel resources must be assigned so that multiple jobs are served in parallel. These modalities are likely to be combined, so that e. g. two rendering jobs can be served at the same time, with both jobs themselves requiring parallel resources to accommodate their datasets. This leads to the following working definition:

Definition 2 (Distributed Volume Rendering) *The term Distributed Volume Rendering unites the notions of parallel volume rendering and multi-user volume rendering. Parallel volume rendering implies data or task parallelism. Data and task parallelism may imply distribution in space and time. Distributed Volume Rendering implies the capability to support simultaneous accesses by multiple users in addition to accesses by single users. Combinations of these ways of utilization are possible.*

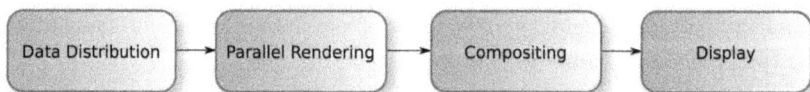

Figure 4.1: Distributed Volume Rendering Pipeline, data distribution and display phase are sequential tasks, while rendering and compositing are usually performed by multiple processors in parallel.

4.2 The Distributed Volume Rendering Pipeline

Pipeline approaches are omnipresent in Computer Graphics and Visualization applications [Bli96] [Mor13]. Pipelines in these contexts usually are an abstraction of the data flow through the execution of a specific algorithm like the rasterization algorithm implemented on modern graphics cards [Pin88], or through a more loosely coupled set of tasks, like the data flow visualization paradigm found in numerous scientific visualization applications [Hen04] [RLL+96]. A GPU-based volume rendering pipeline was proposed by Vollrath et al. [VWE05]. Their publication was oriented towards volume rendering on a single computer with only one GPU and divided the rendering algorithm itself into several stages. Peterka et al. [PRY+08] proposed a parallel volume rendering pipeline. The pipeline approach in their paper is similar to the Distributed Volume Rendering Pipeline proposed by this work, with the main difference being that this work identifies the display phase as an additional pipeline stage. The display phase determines how a remote rendered image is displayed on a remote client. A more thorough investigation of the display phase than the brief one following in the remainder of this chapter can be found in Chapter 6. The remaining stages of the pipeline in Peterka et al. comprised *I/O*, *Render* and *Compositing*, which directly map to the other pipeline stages identified by this work and which are described in detail in the following. Pipeline approaches have the advantage that stages typically are loosely coupled. With loose coupling, program logic from a single stage can be exchanged to implement custom logic, as far as the interface is identical to the original stage regarding the data that flows into and out of the stage.

The pipeline approach proposed by this work is depicted in Figure 4.1. The compositing stage is an optional stage that is only needed with parallel volume rendering and a spatial data distribution. Rendering and compositing are tasks that are usually performed in parallel, while data distribution and display are typically tasks that are assigned to a single processor. The pipeline is optimized for sort-last parallel volume rendering, but sort-first parallel volume rendering could easily be incorporated too.

This work in general follows the pipeline approach specifically because of its simplicity when it comes to specializing the stages of the pipeline. The focus of the architecture is to facilitate the implementation of a visualization system that is capable of running on highly heterogeneous hardware platforms. Usage scenarios comprise real-time applications running in VR, exploration of large datasets on dedicated graphics hardware, or in situ visualization, where the dataset that was e. g. generated as the result of a simulation remains on the cluster used to run the simulation, so that the available hardware must suffice to generate the visualization. The pipeline stages and the way they can be specialized to match the needs of a most versatile system for Distributed Volume Rendering are discussed in further detail in the remainder of this chapter.

4.3   Data Distribution

In case of sort-last volume rendering data distribution requires careful adjustment. Then the dataset is usually divided among the worker nodes to accomplish not just task parallelism, but also data parallelism. In this case, distribution schemes are desired that reduce redundancies in communicating data over the network. With sort-last parallel volume rendering, a visibility sorting data structure such as k-d trees [Ben75] are employed to accomplish a spatial subdivision and assignment of data to the worker nodes. The data distribution task is assigned to a dedicated worker node that also serves as the master node. Usually, this node would also be responsible for synchronization of the compositing stage. Volume data is distributed from the master node to the worker nodes in a top-down fashion. The implementation based on the software architecture makes use of specialization of this stage in two ways.

Parallel File System. The volume dataset is located on a parallel file system that each worker node has access to. Then the master node only needs to distribute the convex bounding object of the volume data to each worker node that it is assigned to, i. e. only the outlines of the k-d tree nodes need to be distributed. With that information, the worker nodes can load their assigned part of the dataset from the file system.

IP Multicast. Like in the parallel file system case, the outlines of the convex bounding objects need to be distributed to the worker nodes by the master node. After that, the master node sends the whole dataset via IP Multicast. The worker nodes sort out their respective pieces of the dataset and store only those permanently.

With the parallel file system approach, the whole network load is imposed on the connection between the nodes and the file server. Multicast is based upon the UDP protocol, so that a reliability layer is necessary to ensure that all the data was received by the worker nodes. To ensure that each datagram reached its recipient, additional meta information needs to be communicated and with the specific implementation, if multicast failed, TCP unicast is used to resend the data to the single node that the multicast failed for. The choice of the appropriate distribution method should be based on practicality reasons such as the size of the dataset, the reliability of the network connecting the nodes, or upon locality in terms of the physical connection between the HPC system and the file server. Allowing for several ways to distribute the volume datasets increases the versatility of the visualization software.

4.4   Generic Parallelization Scheme for Sort-Last Rendering

The generic parallel rendering stage of the Distributed Volume Rendering Pipeline is implemented by means of an abstract renderer interface that each renderer inherits from. That way, the various DVR algorithms described in Section 3.2 can be accommodated as separate renderers.

Remote clients also inherit from the abstract renderer data type. These renderers maintain a network connection to communicate with a remote server instance. This remote server instance itself is capable of running any kind of renderer, uses this to render an image, and returns it to the remote client in response to a rendering request. The specifics behind the network connection are also hidden behind a layer of abstraction, so that e. g. TCP sockets can easily be interchanged for an MPI implementation without affecting the remote server and remote client pair.

Sort-last parallel rendering is supported by the pipeline in a generic fashion by having

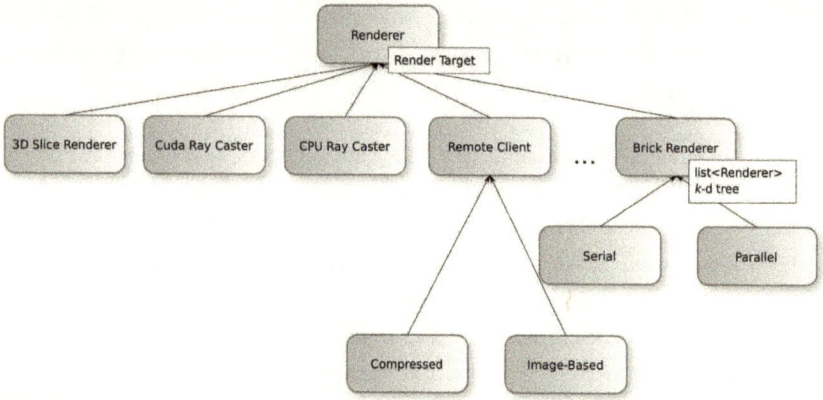

Figure 4.2: Renderer class hierarchy distinguishing between elementary renderers and renderers that indirectly perform volume rendering. Remote renderers connect to remote servers that themselves run arbitrary renderers. Brick renderers provide means for parallelization and handling of large datasets.

a special parallel renderer instance called a *brick renderer*. For sort-last parallel volume rendering, the volume has to be subdivided into convex objects. Such a subdivision is achieved by the brick renderer by partitioning the volume into disjoint bricks that are organized using a k-d tree visibility sorting data structure. The abstract brick renderer maintains the k-d tree. Brick renderers are then derived from by serial and parallel brick renderers. Serial brick renderers store a list of *elementary renderers*, i. e. renderers that directly implement a DVR algorithm, for each leaf of the k-d tree. The k-d tree is then consecutively traversed in back-to-front order and each leaf is processed by the renderer associated with it. That way, out-of-core rendering like it was described in Section 3.2.7 is achieved and volumes can be displayed that do not fit into the video memory of a single graphics card as a whole. Parallel brick renderers also perform back-to-front traversal, but perform processing of the leaf nodes in separate threads. Each thread has a separate renderer. Each thread can possibly have a separate OpenGL® rendering context, that can be scheduled on one of multiple GPUs by means of configuring the thread to GPU affinity using the operating system. Renderers associated with the threads can be elementary renderers or remote clients. If the renderers are remote clients, a distributed memory sort-last parallel volume rendering scenario can be implemented. This hierarchy is arbitrarily extensible in a nested fashion by having e. g. the remote clients themselves running a Multi-GPU configuration or even a distributed memory configuration. The particular software design follows an approach which specifically accommodates sort-last parallel rendering by integrating the spatial data structure for visibility sorting into the architecture. Supporting sort-last is more complicated when it comes to software architectural issues. The main reason for that is the fact that data is distributed among the nodes of the HPC system and a dedicated node is necessary for bookkeeping. The software design, however, is explicitly capable of supporting a setup using sort-first parallel rendering and even combinations of sort-first and sort-last rendering. A concrete implementation of the parallel rendering stage of the Distributed Volume Rendering Pipeline for a combined Multi-GPU and SIMD CPU architecture is proposed and evaluated in Chapter 5. This implementation dedicates basic processing *units* to render data stored at the leafs of the k-d tree used for sort-last, while each basic processing unit itself employs sort-first to render the intermediate image it is responsible for.

4.5 Display Phase

In addition to the pipeline stages from Peterka et al., this work identifies the display phase as a significant means for specialization. This stems from the fact that this work focuses on remote rendering scenarios where the display client process is running on another computer than the render server process.

Having the display phase separated from the preceding rendering stage can be beneficial in many ways. The most simple implementation of the display phase would output the array of colors obtained from the rendering stage to the currently bound rendering context. In addition to that, a more advanced implementation could e. g. upscale the array of colors to match to a higher resolution or redirect the output to a file. The specific implementations that were integrated into the Virvo DVR library are a simple direct rendering display client, a remote rendering display client using image compression, and the image-based remote rendering display client described below in Chapter 6.

4.6   Interactive Resource Management

Interactive visualization applications have special requirements regarding resource management. This work proposes an interactive resource management approach based on zero configuration networking (zeroconf) [SC05]. The interactive resource management approach can handle rendering requests from a multi-user environment. As an extension to that, multiple resources can be assigned to one job. With the flexibility introduced by zeroconf, a job can even be enhanced using additional resources without having to stop the job for reassignment.

4.6.1   One Resource Per User

Figure 4.3 outlines the basic control flow of the resource acquisition procedure. The interactive resource management system is realized as a client-server model. The server-side consists of several remote rendering servers and one resource manager instance. The resource manager serves as the gateway to the remote client instance that implements the display phase of the Distributed Volume Rendering Pipeline. Remote servers can register with the resource manager at any time using zeroconf. A handle to the remote server is then stored in a queue of available resources.

The resource manager can serve requests from multiple users. Requests are paired with interactive resources to jobs. When a job was set up successfully, a network connection is established between the client and the assigned remote server. Rendering events are then passed between remote client and remote server until the network connection is closed. After that, the remote server can be enqueued to the resources queue again. The great benefit of the zeroconf approach is that HPC systems can be enhanced with new resources at run time and that remote servers that are temporarily unavailable e. g. due to maintenance can simply be removed without affecting the whole system.

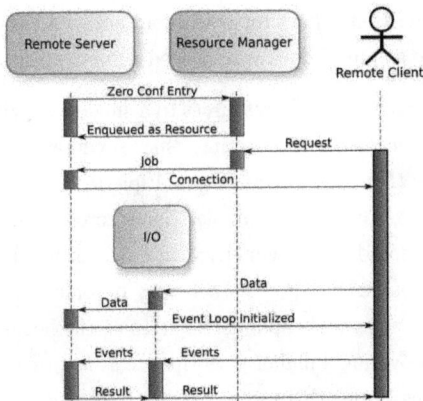

Figure 4.3: Resources register with the resource manager subsystem using a zero configuration networking protocol. The resource manager establishes connections between remote servers and remote clients by pairing requests and resources to jobs.

4.6.2 Multiple Resources Per User

In addition to providing multi-user support, the resource manager can support the allocation of multiple resources to a single user. In that case, one job binds a set of resources to render the dataset in parallel using a brick renderer. In the static case, the acquisition procedure is similar to the case where only one resource is assigned per user. The complexity of having to allocate multiple resources is hidden behind the job and thus opaque to the user, who establishes a network connection with the master process maintaining the k-d tree when the requested amount of resources is available.

While the abstraction implemented by the brick renderers hides the details from the user, the zeroconf approach used by the resource manager is most promising. Although not implemented in the current version of the resource management subsystem of Virvo, in the future the zeroconf approach could be exploited to enable the user to request additional resources at run time. In addition to having to rebuild the k-d tree, the participating resources would need to distribute part of their workload to the newly added resource. In that case, care must be taken that a

k-d tree is constructed that allows for adding an additional node in a fashion that only a fraction of the acquired data would need to be transferred.

In the context of providing multiple resources to a single user with the aid of zeroconf, scheduling would also become an interesting issue. A conservative scheduling strategy would probably imply that a user requiring multiple resources will have to wait until the desired amount of resources is available. Using zeroconf and scaling at run time, scheduling strategies could be implemented that assign fewer resources earlier and provide additional resources to the job when they become available. Such a strategy could be extended to assign less capable resources at the beginning, and exchanging these for more ones providing a higher performance at run time. Although scheduling is out the scope of this thesis, this topic provides tremendous opportunity for future work.

Chapter 5

Implementing the Parallel Rendering Phase of the Distributed Volume Rendering Pipeline

This chapter proposes a concrete implementation of the parallel rendering stage of the Distributed Volume Rendering Pipeline from Chapter 4. The implementation is directed towards many-core systems, which are served using a combination of sort-last and sort-first parallel rendering. Many-core systems can consist of arbitrary processors which can perform rendering tasks. One such family of processors are GPGPUs, which are targeted using a sort-first parallel volume ray casting implementation. CPUs are another constituent of many-core architectures and are targeted using a packet traversal-based SIMD volume ray casting implementation in conjunction with a sort-first multi-core implementation based on a task queue approach. This implementation is feasible for modern CPUs exposing the SSE 4.1 or the AVX instruction set and can even scale to HPC coprocessors like the Intel® Xeon Phi™ by providing code paths specifically designed for the 512 bit wide SIMD instruction set of this hardware. If multiple of the aforementioned processing units are available, their individual results are combined using sort-last rendering. Figure 5.1 provides

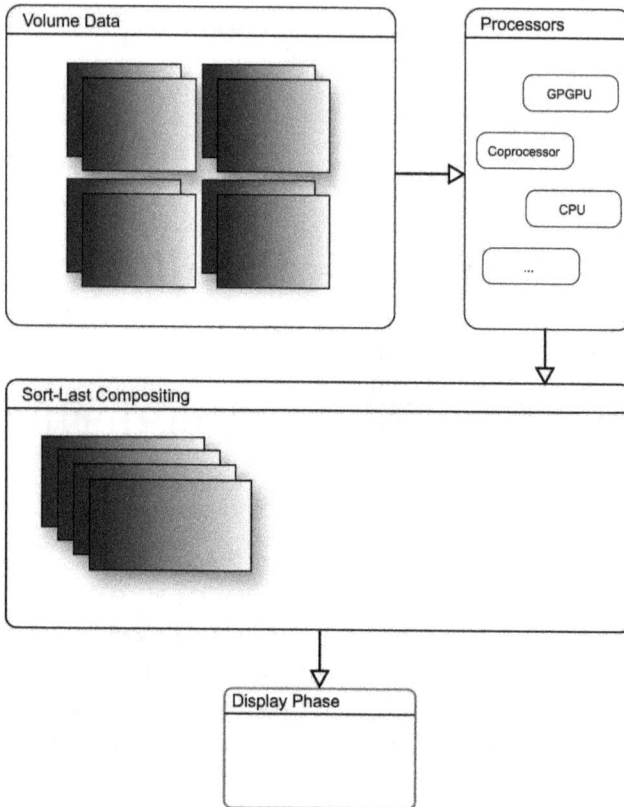

Figure 5.1: Architecture underlying the parallel DVR implementation. The volume dataset is subdivided for sort-last compositing. Chunks of data are served to processors, which implement sort-first parallel volume ray casting. Processors may range from CPUs over GPGPUs to coprocessors like the Intel® Xeon Phi™. Platform specific ray casting code is loaded that is either customized for GPGPUs using NVIDIA® CUDA™, or for Intel® compatible hardware using SIMD instructions. After sort-last compositing, the final image is passed on to the display phase of the Distributed Volume Rendering Pipeline.

an overview of the architecture underlying the parallel rendering implementation.

The chapter is organized as follows. Section 5.1 describes several sort-first DVR implementations that are targeted towards different architectures which are suited for graphics processing to varying degrees. Section 5.2 outlines how the various sort-first implementations are combined using sort-last parallel rendering, and Section 5.3 summarizes their integration into the open source DVR library Virvo. Section 5.4 provides a formal evaluation of the sort-first implementations based on performance measurements. Section 5.5 finally concludes this chapter.

5.1 Sort-First Volume Ray Casting for High Performance Computing Platforms

The ensuing subsections describe concrete implementations for sort-first parallel DVR using ray casting for GPGPU architectures and for CPU architectures. These descriptions are followed by a comparison of the implementations for the various architectures.

5.1.1 GPGPU Volume Ray Casting Implementation

The compute power of GPGPUs is exploited using a parallel ray casting implementation like the one described in Section 3.4.2. The implementation uses the NVIDIA® CUDA™ technology. While Section 3.4.2 outlined the basic principles for parallelizing ray casting on a GPGPU, this section describes a specific implementation.

Ray casting is performed using a single CUDA™ kernel that is called from the host with the current camera and viewing transform as parameters. That way, the most significant part of the ray casting algorithm is executed on the GPGPU, which initially receives the volume, while later on only some control information on how to render the volume for a specific view point is necessary. After the whole ray casting procedure was executed on the device, the rendered color buffer is either transferred back to the host for further processing, or is displayed using pixelbuffer objects which come with CUDA's interoperability layers with the graphics APIs OpenGL® or DirectX®. This approach of having the most compute intensive part of the ray casting algorithm execute on the device minimizes expensive communication over the PCIe interface.

On the device, a persistent thread approach is used to serve threads that are active throughout the rendering job and that process disjoint portions of screen space. This approach effectively balances the workload on devices with inferior scheduling capabilities.

Algorithm 1: Disjoint screen space portions are distributed to warps of persistent CUDA™ threads. The first (or any arbitrarily chosen) thread in the warp uses atomic operations to increment the screen space portion counter. After barrier synchronization, ray casting is performed independently by all threads.

---

1 *counter* ← 0
2 **while** 1 **do**
3   **if** *first thread in warp* **then**
4   *counter* ← *AtomicAdd*(*counter*, 1)
5   **if** *counter* ≥ *maxportions* **then**
6   **return**
7   **end**
8   *portion.xy* ← *ScreenSpacePortion*(*counter*)
9   **end**
10   all threads:
11   *WaitLocalBarrier*()
12   *RayCast*(*portion*)
13 **end**

Figure 5.2 outlines the basic control flow of a single warp of persistent threads. One dedicated thread in the warp queries a task queue maintaining disjoint image space portions. If a portion of image space is left for rendering, the thread increments a counter indicating how many portions of image space are processed. The increment operation must be synchronized among all threads and is implemented using atomic operations (cf. [AL09]). If all portions of image space are processed, the algorithm terminates. Algorithm 1 illustrates this approach using pseudo code. In a

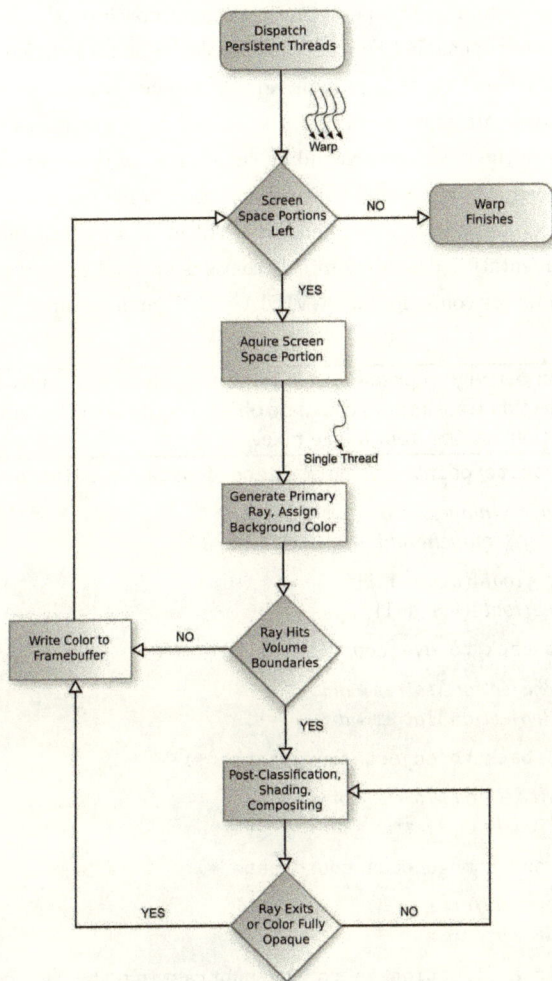

Figure 5.2: Control flow of a single CUDA™ warp implementing a persistent thread approach for volume ray casting. After a portion of screen space is obtained, each thread can independently process a single ray.

technical paper that was published as an addendum to [AL09], Aila et al. [ALK12] investigated the usefulness of a persistent thread approach on the later NVIDIA® GPU architectures codenamed Fermi™ and Kepler™ and concluded that on these architectures persistent threads provide no performance advantage over naive approaches that dedicate fixed amounts of workload to single warps. The authors attributed this to the advanced scheduling capabilities of these later architectures, but also concluded that a persistent thread approach, while not being advantageous on these architectures, on the other hand does not incur a performance *decrease*, so that the implementation described in this thesis is optimal in terms of backwards compatibility, and for contemporary NVIDIA® GPU architectures.

Algorithm 2: Setting up primary rays involves applying the backward model-view and projection transform to calculate object coordinate ray origin positions and ray direction vectors from image pixels.

---

1 (* two opposite points in normalized device coordinates *)

2 $u \leftarrow (thread.x/(imagewidth - 1)) * 2 - 1$
3 $v \leftarrow (thread.y/(imageheight - 1)) * 2 - 1$

4 $ori \leftarrow make\_float4(u, v, -1, 1)$
5 $dir \leftarrow make\_float4(u, v, 1, 1)$

6 (* convert back to eye coordinates *)

7 $ori \leftarrow InvProjectionMatrix * ori$
8 $dir \leftarrow InvProjectionMatrix * dir$

9 (* convert back to object coordinates *)

10 $ori \leftarrow InvModelviewMatrix * ori$
11 $dir \leftarrow InvModelviewMatrix * dir$

12 (* divide out homogeneous coordinate *)

13 $ori.xyz \leftarrow ori.xyz/ori.w$
14 $dir.xyz \leftarrow dir.xyz/dir.w$

15 (* make dir a direction vector by subtracting the two points and
    normalizing *)

16 $dir.xyz \leftarrow dir.xyz - ori.xyz$
17 $normalize(dir.xyz)$

18 $make\_ray(ori.xyz, dir.xyz)$

With the SIMT approach (cf. Section 3.3.4), parallel code for the whole warp is generated implicitly, while only the control flow for a single thread is exposed through the GPU kernel. Thus, the ray casting procedure can be generally described for a single ray, with the CUDA™ compiler generating parallel GPU machine code for the kernel in device code.

Each thread therefore computes a primary ray as follows. First a ray in normalized device coordinates is defined that is perpendicular to the image plane and orthogonal to the screen space position of the image pixel associated with the thread. Then the inverse projection and model-view transform is applied to that ray to obtain a ray having object coordinates. Algorithm 2 outlines this transformation in detail. The image pixel associated with the ray is initially assigned the background color. The ray is then tested for intersection with the bounding box of the volume and is only processed further if the test does not fail. Then all active threads in the warp sample the volume at their current position, perform post-classification with their volume sample and optionally apply a local reflectance model. The obtained color is then blended on top of the already calculated color using alpha compositing. Early-ray termination is performed by testing the composited color for being fully or nearly opaque. If this is not the case, the ray is marched on and then tested for still being originated inside the volume's bounding box. If all rays in the warp finished execution, the color associated with them is assigned to their respective location in the frame buffer memory region. When there are no more screen space portions to process, program execution returns to the host. The image can either directly be displayed on the graphics card, or it is copied to host memory for further processing (the latter being necessary e. g. if sort-last compositing is performed on a GPU other than the one used for ray casting).

The CUDA™ implementation makes tremendous use of C++ template programming to shift run time decisions to compile time. E. g. the decision whether the optional reflection calculations should be performed, is made by compiling two separated device kernels, one with the shading branch enabled and the other one compiled without the shading branch. Based on the users choice, the appropriate kernel is then loaded at run time, before the volume dataset is loaded. This approach on the one hand guarantees run time efficiency, but on the other hand can result in high compilation times and an increased size of the compiled binary containing the ray casting kernels.

Because there is no branch prediction for code executed by the threads in a single warp, it is mandatory to avoid divergence of the code paths. Ray casting of structured volume data is especially benign regarding branch divergence. The only dynamic branches in the ray casting code involve tests for the ray actually hitting the volume, as well as tests for the ray exiting the volume. In both cases, for nearby rays the probability is high that if one ray passes the test, all the rays that are processed in a packet pass the test. In general, the more threads are traced through the volume in a single warp, the higher the probability that some threads miss one of the tests, are thus marked inactive early and cannot contribute during the remaining computation. If warps are underutilized due to many inactive threads, one approach could be to reassign work to single threads from different warps during execution. Wald [Wal11] investigated techniques he called *warp compaction* for ray tracing, just to find out that reorganizing warps for better utilization is not beneficial on current GPGPU hardware. Underutilized SIMT warps nevertheless are more problematic e. g. in surface ray tracing scenarios, which typically involve stochastic sampling and highly divergent secondary rays, which are generated to evaluate phenomena like soft shadows or glossy reflection. The DVR algorithm implemented for the purposes of this thesis, anyhow, is based on traversing coherent rays through the volume density, so that warp underutilization in general is a less imminent problem compared to warp underutilization in Monte Carlo ray tracing.

5.1.2   Sort-First Parallel Volume Ray Casting for Multi-Core Systems

With the NVIDIA® CUDA™-based implementation, the workload distribution among SMs is performed via persistent threads and a task queue approach, while the SIMT units are programmed implicitly. Programming Intel®-compatible CPUs requires similar considerations. Modern Intel®-compatible CPUs are multi-core CPUs, with programmable SIMD units having a word length of 128 to 256 bit pertaining to each CPU core [FBJ+08]. To efficiently utilize the hardware, applications must

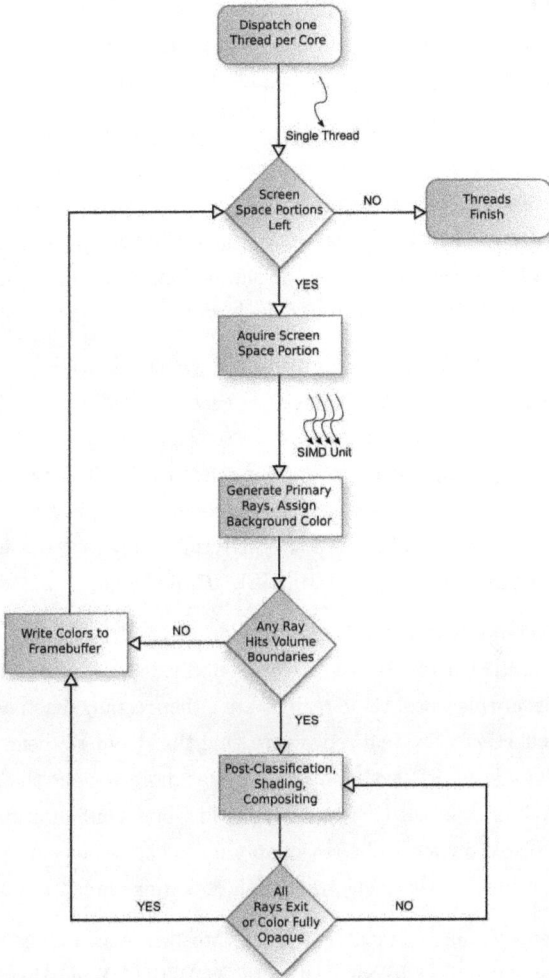

Figure 5.3: Control flow for the ray casting algorithm implemented on a multi-core CPU. One thread is launched per CPU core. Threads retrieve screen space portions from a task queue and process them using the SIMD unit and packet ray casting.

incorporate multi-core- as well as SIMD parallelism. The remainder of this subsection illustrates how the ray casting workload is distributed to the cores of a multi-core CPU. Figure 5.3 outlines the control flow of *ray packets* that are used to traverse the volume dataset. Ray packets unify neighboring rays into a *slab*.

Screen space decomposition is performed using a two-level approach. First of all, screen space is subdivided into disjoint regions that are served to the cores of the CPU. These regions themselves are then further subdivided to be processed by the SIMD units of the CPU cores by traversing them using ray packets. While the ray packet traversal is covered by the ensuing subsection, this subsection concentrates on the screen space decomposition and distribution on the multi-core level.

Knoll et al. [KTW+11] in their CPU-based DVR system referred to the screen space regions that are served to the CPU cores as *"packets"*, while they called the SIMD packets, which in general form a subset of the screen space regions, *"packlets"*. This thesis does not adopt this nomenclature but refers to the data passed to the CPU cores as *screen space regions* or *screen space portions*, and to the subset served to the SIMD units as *packets*. By this, it follows the terminology that was highly adopted by the ray tracing literature [WSBW01] [BEL+07] [ORM08].

Screen space decomposition and distribution on the multi-core level is based on a task queue approach. For that, screen space is subdivided into small, disjoint regions. For the purposes of this work, these regions are either rectangular tiles or horizontal stripes, which effectively are realized by creating tiles having a height of one pixel. In general, on modern CPU systems there are far more regions than threads that can be scheduled on different CPU cores, e. g. for some configurations tiles with a size of 16×16 pixels proved to be reasonably fast. The regions are then enqueued into a globally available task queue, that each rendering thread has access to.

With this implementation, as many rendering threads are created as there are CPU cores. Each thread is *pinned* to one CPU core [KOWT11]. Rendering commands are issued to the threads via an event-based system. When the task queue was filled with screen space regions and the rendering command was issued to an individual thread, that one retrieves one region from the task queue and starts processing it using its SIMD units. After each ray packet traversal, the thread writes its computed pixel colors to the respective positions in a global array of colors. When all screen space regions were processed, the global array of colors is used to fill the frame buffer.

As there are usually far more screen space regions than there are rendering threads, this approach balances the workload among the rendering threads since the assignment of screen space regions to threads is performed dynamically. The implemented load-balancing scheme is a common one for parallel real-time graphics. A similar approach, although applied to surface ray tracing and based on a cost estimate, was e. g. recently proposed by Cosenza et al. [CDE13] (cf. Section 3.4.4).

5.1.3 SIMD-Based Ray Casting Kernel for Intel®-Compatible CPUs

This subsection describes how to optimize volume ray casting for Intel®-compatible CPUs. In general, nevertheless, many of the remarks e. g. regarding ray packet layouts and the description of the wrapper classes for vector intrinsics also apply to the ensuing Subsection 5.1.4, which describes optimizations for the Intel® Xeon Phi™ architecture, which are to a significant degree derived from the considerations made in this subsection.

With SIMD-based volume ray casting, in contrast to programming the SIMT units of the NVIDIA®
GPGPUs in terms of the execution of a single threads, the SIMD parallelism must be programmed explicitly. With this implementation, that is achieved by traversing ray packets instead of single rays through the volume dataset. Ray packets lend themselves especially well to SIMD implementations, because a single operation like a dot product or a normalization routine for direction vectors can be executed upon the whole packet instead of upon a single ray [WSB01]. Ray packets are especially useful because of spatial coherence that can be exploited by traversing adjacent rays through the volume. On architectures that gain their speed advantages through a sophisticated cache organization, coherence considerations are crucial.

When implementing the SIMD ray packet traversal algorithm, several levels of abstraction need to be considered which typically trade computation cost for portability.

Most explicit programming of the SIMD units results in the highest control over register usage and instruction utilization, at the cost of highly unportable code.

The highest level of control can be reached when explicitly programming with the machine code instructions provided by the targeted instruction set. On Intel® -compatible CPUs, one can e. g. use the SIMD extensions SSE or AVX [FBJ+08]. When explicitly programming using the vector instructions using inline assembly code, the programmer has to take care of register usage, which involves explicitly programming the control flow in terms of loading of data items to and from specific vector registers.

Intel® enables a slightly higher abstraction level by providing so called *vector intrinsics* (cf. Section 3.3.1). Intrinsics wrap vector instructions using C-functions and provide vector data types that fit into one register of the SIMD vector units provided by the CPU. Depending on the architecture of the targeted instruction set, the SIMD width of a vector amounts to 128 bits for SSE, 256 bits for AVX or 512 bits for the native instruction set of the Intel® Xeon Phi™ coprocessor card. Being able to program with pseudo high-level programming language variables that the C-function wrappers operate upon, the programmer does not have to explicitly load data items to and from the vector registers. Load- and store instructions are generated by the compiler. This facilitates high-level access to SIMD programming with vector instructions, but can result in less efficient register usage. The overall behavior can be fine-tuned in an ensuing profiling step, e. g. by changing the order of certain vector instructions to help the compiler to generate more efficient code. Intrinsics enable the programmer to use high-level constructs such as loops. The programmer does not need to *explicitly* care to only use a certain number of registers or to spill register content if too many registers are in use. She also does not need to store and restore state before and after function calls. Nevertheless, fine-tuning is usually necessary for the compiler-generated code.

Programming ray tracing-based algorithms with SIMD instructions typically implies most of the data structures involved to be organized as *Structures of Arrays* (SoA) instead of *Arrays of Structures* (AoS) [KTW+11]. SoA ray traversal is implemented by packing rays together into a common data structure called a *packet*. With that, a

---

Algorithm 3: Ray packet as Array of Structures vs. ray packets as Structure of Arrays.

```
1  (* AoS packet *)
2  struct ray
3      float ox, oy, oz
4      float dx, dy, dz
5  endstruct
6  ray packet[N]
7  -----------------------
8  (* SoA packet *)
9  struct ray_packet
10     float ox[N], oy[N], oz[N]
11     float dx[N], dy[N], dz[N]
12 endstruct
13 ray_packet packet
```

---

group of *coherent* rays can be traversed through the volume that is likely to interact with the same grid cells. This traversal scheme promises better cache utilization and more coherent memory access patterns in general, which for large datasets is crucial to the overall performance of the ray casting algorithm.

The approach of organizing data structures to contain arrays instead of single data items tends to be less readable for humans but can help the compiler during optimization. Invoked with flags hinting the compiler to optimize serial code using the vector units, vector instructions can be generated without explicitly using them or their intrinsic equivalents. This feature which is called "auto-vectorization" is supported by all modern compilers known to the author. Efficient vector instructions can only be generated by the auto-vectorizer if the code is organized in a fashion that hints the compiler how to translate the serial code into SIMD code. If the arrays contained in the data structure e. g. have a length corresponding to the SIMD width of the instruction set that is used, and if their first memory address is aligned in accordance to the targeted instruction set, the compiler is able to produce an efficient mapping of the arrays to vector registers. Arithmetic or comparison operations performed on SoA variables can be translated to vector operations by the compiler. Typically, if complicated constructs like loops grow more complicated, the likelihood that the compiler can auto-vectorize the code decreases. In general, constructs like dependent loop iterations are of course prohibitive because the auto-vectorizer relies on loop unrolling so that e. g. four iterations can be flattened to a single iteration using vector arithmetic. Writing code that is auto-vectorizable can be quite cumbersome. While the use of intrinsics or even assembler instructions implies that new instruction sets must be targeted with platform-specific code, the same is true, although less obvious, if one relies on the auto-vectorization feature of the compiler. In that case, special care has to be taken that efficient SIMD code is generated on all platforms by any compiler. Under the worst conditions, if no special care is taken, code will be generated that implies context switches where data is swapped from vector registers to general-purpose registers, which is prohibitive in terms of efficiency. The author argues that anyway, if optimized code is ported to a new platform, adjustments are necessary, independent of whether vectorization is achieved implicitly by using auto-vectorization or explicitly by using intrinsics or assembler code.

When DVR is implemented using ray casting, candidates for SoA implementations are the ray packets (cf. Algorithm 3). When storing ray packets as AoS, compilers will typically pack at most the x, y and z component of the origin points and direction vectors into one vector register, respectively. This will result in a low register utilization that becomes more infeasible with growing SIMD widths that come with newer hardware architectures. On top of that, if ray packets are stored that way, the ray traversal algorithm can only slightly benefit from parallel vector operations. Consider e. g. the normalization operation for a single direction vector $D = (D_x, D_y, D_z)$:

$$D = \frac{D}{\sqrt{D_x^2 + D_y^2 + D_z^2}},\qquad(5.1)$$

where the terms to the second power are of course computed using a single multiplication. Assuming that this operation is applied to an array of N' 3D vectors, without optimizations applied, the floating-point unit (FPU) will require N' times three multiplications, two additions, one square root operation and three divisions to compute this equation. For simplicity's sake, in the following it will be assumed that each of these instructions have the same latency. Without optimization, normalizing a direction vector would thus take N' times nine floating-point instructions. With AoS ray packets, the compiler could e. g. translate this operation to exploit vector parallelism in the following way:

$$D[n] = \frac{D[n]}{\sqrt{D[n] \cdot D[n]}}, \forall n \in \{0, 1, ..., N - 1\}, \tag{5.2}$$

where N is the SIMD width of the targeted instruction set, and $\cdot$ is a vector operation mapping to a SIMD instruction that computes the dot product of the two vector arguments (such an instruction is e. g. available on Intel® CPUs supporting the SSE 4.1 instruction set). Translated to an actual programming language, this layout will require a loop over the N elements of the vector, while N times three multiplications and two additions can be substituted by N dot product vector instructions. Assuming that the dot product vector instruction has the same latency as the square root and the arithmetic instructions, this optimization will result in N times five vector instructions. With an SoA layout, normalization could be performed as follows:

$$D[N] = \frac{D[N]}{\sqrt{D[N]_x^2 + D[N]_y^2 + D[N]_z^2}}, \tag{5.3}$$

with all arithmetic operations as well as the square root and the assignment being vector instructions and $D[N]$ being a four-vector, where each $D[N]_x$, $D[N]_y$ and $D[N]_z$ are SIMD vectors. Note that now, there is no need to loop over an array of N vectors, because the SIMD operations are executed on arrays of size N. Neglecting the assignment operation, this layout yields nine vector instructions in total. Given an N of e. g. 4, as this is the case when targeting SSE, this compares to 20 instructions for the AoS layout.

The calculation from above is of course only meant for illustration and cannot provide a *realistic* estimate of the actual instruction count incurred by either of the two memory access patterns. Real processors typically implement instruction pipelines and use out-of-order execution to reorder instructions for better pipeline utilization, so that an *absolute* comparison of the instruction count incurred by a specific memory access pattern is in general not meaningful.

Using an SoA layout for the ray packet data structure will provide the compiler with sufficient hints to generate efficiently vectorized code, even if vectorization is not performed explicitly. On top of that, using SoA layouts will in general lead to more highly optimized code. Initialization e. g. is a more efficient operation if a contiguous region of memory is assigned to a vector register through an optimized "*memcpy*" routine rather than using shuffle operations. Apart from merely resulting in a reduced instruction overhead, the most important benefit probably stems from the fact that an SoA layout yields better cache utilization, especially in the context of packet ray casting. Neighboring rays are likely to access the same or at least nearby memory locations, especially if trilinear interpolation is involved where a tight neighborhood of voxels is sampled at a specific position along a ray.

Despite the ubiquity of auto-vectorization features offered by most compilers, for the purposes of the implementation presented in this thesis, an approach based on vector intrinsics is used. This decision was made because the author has the opinion that highly optimized code must be *ported* to new hardware platform for efficiencies sake, and because being explicit about the very instructions that the code is compiled to, finer optimizations are possible that will yield more highly optimized code than this is achievable using auto-vectorization. On the other hand, in order to be able to program in a high-level fashion and to share code between the various SIMD implementations, the intrinsics are wrapped using vector math classes (cf. Algorithm 4). Those can be used to implement ray packets (cf. Algorithm 5). Using the ANSI C *typedef* facility on the type of the SIMD vector enables portability to alternative vector instruction sets. This can be accomplished by using a compile time define so that the type *simd_vec* masquerades as an alternative vector type, and by using intrinsics from the alternative instruction set to implement the operators and vector functions.

Programming with the wrapper classes is then mainly analogous to programming

---

Algorithm 4: Vector math class using SSE vectors in a SoA fashion to mimic scalar vector math data types. Two-vector or four-vector classes are designed in conceptually the same way.

```
1 (* map __m128 SSE vector type to a platform-independent name *)
2 typedef __m128 simd_vec

3 operator+(simd_vec a, simd_vec b)
4     return _mm_add_ps(a, b)
5 end

6 (* SoA three-vector *)

7 struct vec3
8     simd_vec x
9     simd_vec y
10    simd_vec z

11 endstruct

12 operator+(vec3 a, vec3 b)
13    (* use operator+ from above *)
14    return vec3(a.x + b.x, a.y + b.y, a.z + b.z)
15 end

16 (* more operators *)
17 (* ... *)

18 dot(vec3 a, vec3 b)
19    return a.x*b.x + a.y*b.y + a.z*b.z
20 end

21 normalize(vec3 a)
22    return a / sqrt(dot(a,a))
23 end

24 (* more functions *)
25 (* ... *)
```

Algorithm 5: Ray packets using SoA vec3's. The interface of the packet can be used similarly to that of a single ray.

---

1 **struct** ray_packet

2   vec3 ori
3   vec3 dir

4 **endstruct**

Algorithm 6: Primary ray packets are set up analogously to single primary rays as outlined in Algorithm 2, except that N pixel positions are necessary for initialization that span the whole region the packet is responsible for.

---

1 (* SIMD vectors *)
2 simd_vec x, y, u, v
3 vec4 *ori, dir*

4 (* for SSE, PixelPositions e. g. returns the array
   [(x,y),(x+1,y),(x,y+1),(x+1,y+1)] *)
5 $(x, y) \leftarrow PixelPositions(thread.xy)$

6 (* two opposite points in normalized device coordinates *)
7 $u \leftarrow (x/(imagewidth - 1)) * 2 - 1$
8 $v \leftarrow (y/(imageheight - 1)) * 2 - 1$

9 $ori \leftarrow make\_float4(u, v, -1, 1)$
10 $dir \leftarrow make\_float4(u, v, 1, 1)$

11 (* ray packet setup analogous to single ray setup *)
12 (* ... *)

Algorithm 7: Wrapper functions for arithmetic SIMD intrinsics. Binary operators can be wrapped using operator overloading, while ternary, masked arithmetic operators must be wrapped using ordinary (inline) function calls. Calling the binary operators is far more legible.

---

1 (* binary add operation *)

2 simd_vec **operator+**(simd_vec a, simd_vec b)

3   **return** _mm_add_ps(a, b)

4 **end**

5 simd_vec add(simd_vec a, simd_vec b, simd_vec mask)

6   simd_vec $ifexpr \leftarrow a + b$

7   (* masked vector component gets 0 *)

8   simd_vec $elseexpr \leftarrow 0$

9   (* if/else SIMD vector construct *)

10   **return** _mm_or_ps(_mm_and_ps($mask, ifexpr$), _mm_andnot_ps($mask, elseexpr$))

11 **end**

12 (* call to binary operators *)

13 simd_vec $e \leftarrow a + b + c + d$

14 (* analogous call to ternary operators with mask *)

15 simd_vec $f \leftarrow add(add(add(a, b, inactive), c, inactive), d, inactive)$

---

a scalar version of the ray casting algorithm, except for the code sections where the rays are set up or where data is accessed, e. g. to read from the volume data array or to write colors to the color array. When processing a screen space region, this region is further subdivided into subregions that match the SIMD width of the targeted processor. These subregions are then processed sequentially. Ray packets are initialized as outlined in Algorithm 6, which is analogous to Algorithm 2 from the previous subsection, despite that packets are initialized with the screen space positions of a set of pixels instead of only a single pixel. If a ray exits the volume or has gathered enough opacity so that the threshold that was set for early-ray termination is reached, that ray is marked inactive. In contrast to single ray traversal, ray packet traversal continues while *any* of the rays in the packet is active. Inactive rays are marked as inactive by using bitwise masks. This can lead to underutilization especially if the traversal patterns of the rays differ significantly.

Nevertheless, using ray casting to evaluate the absorption plus emission model, where no secondary rays are generated, ray traversal tends to be quite coherent because of the regularity of the access pattern and of the grids that are traversed. That said, having to scale to wider SIMD units means having to traverse wider ray packets, where the probability to suffer from underutilization in general grows. Providing a measure of the degree to which one can scale the ray casting algorithm using SIMD is a research problem not sufficiently tackled so far.

Masked arithmetic operations require functions to be called that take three arguments. In addition to the two operands that the arithmetic operation is performed upon, the mask itself must be passed to the operator. While e. g. the SIMD intrinsic architecture for the Intel® Xeon Phi™ natively supports ternary intrinsic functions (cf. Subsection 5.1.4), the masking behavior must be emulated for SSE by using *if-else* constructs of the form

$$(mask \wedge ifexpr) \vee (mask \wedge \neg elseexpr).$$

Algorithm 8 shows how a masked addition can be realized using an if-else construct that sets the masked out SIMD-vector components of the result to 0.

Algorithm 8: Emulating masked SIMD-operations.

1 simd_vec **if_else**(simd_vec ifexpr, simd_vec elseexpr, mask m)
2   return _mm_or_ps(_mm_and_ps(m, ifexpr), _mm_andnot_ps(m, elseexpr))
3 **end**

4 simd_vec **add**(simd_vec a, simd_vec b, mask m)
5   return if_else(a + b, 0, m)
6 **end**

Since calling *native* masked intrinsics and their analogs taking two operands imposes the same latency, using intrinsics taking two operands whenever possible is preferred for reasons of legibility. Calling intrinsics taking two operands can be wrapped by overloading the appropriate arithmetic operator. However, masked intrinsics cannot be wrapped that way in C++, which only supports a single ternary operator that cannot be overloaded for arithmetic calculations. The inner loop of the ray casting algorithm for uniform grids is divided into a general traversal step to determine the *source* color at a specific sample position, and a compositing step that blends the source color with the *destination* color. If masked SIMD instructions and their ordinary counterparts have the same latency, masked operations must only be used for the compositing step, so that an (invalid) source color is actually computed for masked out rays, while the final color is not affected by the computations.

Several authors reported that *swizzling* can be advantageous for more coherent cache accesses [HKRS+06] [KTW+11]. Swizzling is a cache coherence pattern that reorganizes the volume data. While the texture memory layouts of GPUs in general are not known by the developers due to the hardware vendors not publishing detailed descriptions, CPU memory is known to be organized sequentially. If the memory layout that is used to store the volume follows a scanline order, cache misses for coherent memory accesses are likely. If, in contrast to that, the voxels contained in *bricks* are flattened and then stored in scanlines, memory access patterns will be more coherent. In addition to that, the stride with which the data is accessed is independent of the coordinate axis that is most parallel to the viewing direction. In theory, pairing this data locality strategy with space-filling curves is a promising approach. During the course of this thesis, swizzling was implemented and tested informally. The outcome was however less promising than the literature suggested. A more formal analysis of the impact of this cache locality strategy thus remains future work.

5.1.4   SIMD-Based Ray Casting Kernel for Intel® Xeon Phi™ Coprocessors

The ray casting implementation for the Intel® Xeon Phi™ coprocessor is largely based on the implementation for x86 processors with SIMD vector units from the previous subsection. A detailed description of the coprocessor and its underlying MIC architecture can be found in Section 3.3.5.

Most implementations will favor an offload approach over a native implementation of the ray casting algorithm for the Xeon Phi™ coprocessor, and the implementation proposed hereby will make no exception to this. Ray casting fortunately lends itself quite well to an offload implementation because essentially only those parts of the execution need to be performed on the host that provide control information or that are responsible for displaying the frame buffer. In its current state, the coprocessor is connected to the host over the PCIe interface, so that communication to and from the device incurs the performance bottleneck with the highest impact. The benefit from having most parts of the ray casting algorithm execute on the device and thus reducing communication overhead is thus rather not debatable. This assumption, nevertheless, would not be that evident if the ray tracing kernel would contain dynamic branching that results in incoherent ray traversal. The overhead of maintaining a stack in device memory was investigated e. g. in [BWW+01], and the authors presented an efficient BVH traversal implementation for the wide SIMD units of the MIC architecture. Their findings suggest that even ray traversal algorithms with a high degree of dynamic branching can be efficiently implemented as offload code without additional communication with the host. The offload approach thus strongly resembles the CUDA™ implementation outlined earlier, which performs the same algorithmic parts on the device that are also performed on the coprocessor. In contrast to the GPU implementation, nevertheless, copying the frame buffer back to

the host CPU after rendering is mandatory because the coprocessor is not equipped
with a graphics output.

For the implementation of the offload algorithm, an explicit data copy approach
based on annotation through directives was favored over a shared memory approach
between host and device using Cilk Plus^{TM}. Threads are created once on the device
and pointers to on-device shared memory regions, such as the color buffer, the volume
data, the transfer function, or viewing matrices, are initialized for each thread. The
ray casting algorithm is thus initiated on the host CPU, which copies the color
buffer and the current camera matrix to the shared memory of the coprocessor and
activates the rendering threads by means of synchronization using condition variables.
Although the x86 CPU implementation and the coprocessor implementation have
a common code base, copying is of course only performed when the coprocessor is
involved. The algorithm then proceeds similarly to the CPU algorithm by requesting
screen space portions and rendering them independently.

Algorithm 9: The SIMD vector classes are shared by the implementations.
For that, only the appropriate base instructions must be chosen at compile
time.

```
1 simd_vec operator+(simd_vec a, simd_vec b)
2 #ifdef SSE
3     (* SSE code path *)
4     return _mm_add_ps(a, b)
5 #elif defined MIC
6     (* MIC code path *)
7     return _mm512_add_ps(a, b)
8 #endif
9 end
```

The main difference between the two implementations are the number of threads
on the one hand, and the different SIMD width on the other hand. The task queue
based ray casting implementation in general scales to the 240 threads that can be
scheduled concurrently on the Xeon Phi^{TM} coprocessor the author of this thesis
has access to. The SSE SIMD code, on the other hand, cannot be executed by
the coprocessor and must thus be rewritten using the 512 bit SIMD instructions
that the MIC architecture provides. Apart from the differing SIMD widths, the two

instruction sets also differ because the MIC architecture provides masked instructions. Because the vector wrapper classes proposed above are designed to accommodate both native and emulated masked instructions (cf. Section 5.1.3), reusing the vector classes is simply a matter of deciding for the appropriate instruction set architecture (ISA) at compile time (cf. Algorithm 9).

Algorithm 10: Optimized RGBA texture lookups for SSE and MIC. In both cases, it is beneficial to store the transfer function as AoS. With SSE, this allows for only one store instruction. With the MIC architecture, the expensive context switch can be avoided altogether by using gather intrinsics that implement incoherent memory access in hardware.

---

1 typedef simd_veci index_t
2 vec4 **rgba**(index_t idx)
3 #**ifdef** SSE
4   (* Store indices to general-purpose registers *)
5   **int** indices[4] ←**store**(idx)
6   vec4 color(lut[indices[0]], lut[indices[1]], lut[indices[2]], lut[indices[3]])
7   (* Colors are stored as AoS => transpose *)
8   **return** transpose(color)
9 #**elif defined** MIC
10   (* Simplified gather, intrinsic calls are actually more
        complicated due to conversion and scaling parameters *)
11   simd_vec r = _mm512_i32extgather_ps(idx, lut)
12   simd_vec g = _mm512_i32extgather_ps(idx + 1, lut)
13   simd_vec b = _mm512_i32extgather_ps(idx + 2, lut)
14   simd_vec a = _mm512_i32extgather_ps(idx + 3, lut)
15   **return** vec4(r, g, b, a)
16 #**endif**
17 **end**

Nevertheless, the MIC ISA provides some instructions that are exclusive to the MIC architecture and can be useful for the ray casting implementation. On the one hand, there are so called non-temporal load and store instructions and prefetch instructions that control how and when data is written to the cache before and after it was accessed [KKC+13]. Furthermore, gather and scatter instructions were introduced with the MIC ISA which are specifically useful to implement the post-classification phase of the ray casting algorithm. The rays in a packet are likely to not reconstruct the same values during traversal. Since these values are then reinterpreted as indices into the tabulated transfer function, those lookup table accesses are thus incoherent. On the CPU, the only solution to this is to store all reconstructed indices to general-purpose registers, lookup the appropriate values from the transfer function table and restore those to SIMD floating-point registers. With the MIC architecture, this operation can be implemented using a single gather instruction, which is illustrated in Algorithm 10. Accessing the 3D volume texture can also be optimized by using gather instructions. Note that the signature of the actual gather intrinsic is a bit more verbose than the code listing suggests. Specifically, the actual intrinsics take arguments that allow to specify the source type that is upconverted to a 32 bit floating point number. This can be used to support volumes like the carp dataset used for the tests below in Section 5.4, which consist of 16 bit data items rather than 8 bit data items.

5.1.5 Comparison of the Sort-First Ray Casting Implementations

The ray casting implementations described above, although having a common code base, actually differ regarding their fitness to certain use cases as well as the expectations one may have regarding the performance that is achievable with the different implementations. GPUs, while prevalent in the HPC community nowadays, nevertheless are commodity hardware which is used to equip graphic workstations that are e. g. used by designers or artists. Anyway, even mobile GPUs like the ones that are shipped with notebooks are quite potent, share technology with their HPC counterparts and their counterparts from the professional segment, and can in general be programmed using CUDA^{TM}.

Coprocessors like the Intel® Xeon Phi^{TM} on the other hand are targeted towards HPC systems and are usually not found in commodity systems. Thus, the two implementations, the one targeted towards GPGPUs and the one targeted towards Intel® coprocessors, though structurally similar and based on the same code, in general serve quite different purposes. While GPUs are omnipresent, the Intel® Xeon Phi^{TM} code path is especially interesting for in situ visualization scenarios where the HPC system is equipped with several coprocessor nodes. Thus, while one typical usage scenario for the GPU implementation will be direct rendering, the implementation for the Intel® Xeon Phi™ will typically be used in a remote rendering scenario.

The main advantage of the CPU implementation stems from the fact that the ray casting algorithm can make use of the full amount of CPU main memory on the one hand, and of the CPU's intricate cache architecture on the other hand. In addition to that, no offloading procedure is needed, so that the latency and the limited bandwidth of the PCIe interconnect are not an issue for this code path either.

GPGPUs are traditionally optimized for high throughput. This stems from the historical roots of those systems. GPUs were from the beginning on designed to provide fixed-functionality to process large amounts of vertices or fragments occupying image pixels in parallel. Although with programmable shaders in general and with the unified shader architectures specifically, this rigidity was partly mitigated, GPUs remain at their strongest when being served homogeneous workloads at a high rate. This makes algorithms like DVR especially well suited for those architectures. DVR calculations like computing the volume rendering integral of individual rays can be performed independently. On top of that, the DVR implementation can make use of several features such as hardware-based trilinear interpolation or optimized 3D texture access, that must be implemented using many instructions and that needs to be specifically optimized for memory accesses on CPU platforms.

In general, the main difference between the CUDA™ implementation and the CPU implementation, apart from hardware support for trilinear texture interpolation, is that the CPU implementation is based on packets, and the GPU implementation is not. Section 5.1.3 nevertheless showed that SIMD ray packet traversal can be implemented to *mimic* single-ray traversal by the use of C/C++ language constructs. Aila and Laine [AL09] evaluated packet traversal versus CUDA™ kernels traversing only a single ray and found the latter to be superior. The author of this thesis nevertheless argues that even when traversing a single ray per CUDA™ kernel, the general control flow, where threads are organized in warps and the execution of all threads halts if only a single thread reaches a branch that the other threads do not enter, strongly resembles packet traversal, anyway. The same performance implications have to be considered for rays in a packet that are inactive due to masking and for rays on the GPU that do not participate in the execution of a dynamic branch. However, the CUDA™ *programming model* is more flexible, because it can scale to various warp sizes without having to rewrite the actual kernel. Commonalities in the form of implicit vectorization on GPUs, and in the form of design patterns for SIMD code to masquerade as code acting on single data items, exist, although they are not immediately obvious.

5.2 Sort-Last Implementation for Many-Core Systems

Sort-last rendering is used when the DVR is executed algorithm on *many-core systems*. Many-core systems in this case subsume two specific types of computer systems: on the one hand *clusters* of computers connected via a network, and on the other hand Multi-GPU systems, where GPUs are connected over PCIe. This allows for quite heterogeneous configurations because a cluster node can itself be a Multi-GPU system. In such a system, atomic units are either single accelerators like GPUs, or a group of CPU cores in a node. With the proposed configuration, each atomic unit executes one of the sort-first code paths described above on a subset of the volume dataset. The contributions from the various atomic units are then combined using sort-last compositing.

Sort-last rendering is initialized by first finding an appropriate data partitioning and then organizing the resulting volume blocks using a k-d tree. The k-d tree is maintained by a parallel brick renderer like it was described in Section 4.4. On a Multi-GPU system, one thread per GPU is committed to sending control information and downloading the color buffer. With the network solution, each node runs a separate instance of the DVR library (cf. Section 5.3). In any case, each of those asynchronous computational units renders the share of the volume that was assigned to it concurrently. Compositing is started when all units reached a synchronization barrier. Compositing itself is performed by traversing the k-d tree according to the current viewing position.

Compositing was implemented using a simple approach where whole images are sent to a compositing node. This approach is known to scale badly because it imposes severe network contention when many processors are involved. However, for the common scenario with at most four GPUs in one node, the compositing phase did not prove to be a bottleneck. For use cases with more processors involved, this observation will likely not hold true. In order to support general use cases, having an implementation based on one of the compositing algorithms described in Section 3.4.3, probably by using a library for compositing, would be more desirable. Sort-last rendering with DVR is a well-understood problem. This thesis therefore does not include an evaluation of this implementation. A formal analysis of sort-last DVR on a cluster can be found in Bajaj et al. [BPT02], while an analysis of sort-last DVR on Multi-GPU systems was conducted by Marchesin et al. [MMD08].

5.3   Integration into the Direct Volume Rendering Library Virvo

The parallel implementations were integrated into the DVR library Virvo (cf. Section 3.5.3). Since both DeskVOX as well as COVISE use this library for DVR, both visualization systems can benefit from the parallelization. This section gives a technical overview of the integration into the Virvo library.

The various sort-first ray casting implementations were integrated using Virvo's plugin mechanism that can load dynamic code at run time. This is convenient since that way the most efficient instruction set can be chosen dynamically based on the available configuration. The configuration is tested at run time for the availability of accelerators like a GPGPU or an Intel® Xeon Phi™, and for the availability of SSE or AVX using the CPUID instruction [Int13].

Sort-last parallel Multi-GPU rendering was integrated into the Virvo library by means of the abstraction layer described in Section 4.4 and is available on platforms that support an X server with the GLX protocol [LWK05]. Each GPU is then associated with a separate GLX window or a GLX Pbuffer, which is bound to a specific GPU via configuration, e. g. by running one X server per GPU or by configuring only one X server, but with two X displays as a parent to the GLX window. With NVIDIA® CUDA™, it is in general possible to bind a task to a specific GPU by means of a simple API call. However, the implementation via the GLX protocol was chosen to implement the parallel rendering stage of the Distributed Volume Rendering Pipeline in a most generic way. By associating the rendering modules with their respective GPU via configuration, renderers can be accommodated that are not implemented using CUDA™. This makes the sort-last rendering algorithm reusable e. g. for the texture-based rendering code paths that are also implemented as part of the Virvo library. CPU execution does not have to be explicitly bound to an X server or X display if running on the local machine. Similarly, this it is not necessary for the Intel® Xeon Phi™ coprocessor. These rendering modules may share the X server and even the X display with one of the other rendering modules. In practice, and if the viewing context allows for direct rendering, with the current implementation these modules actually run in a thread that has access to the viewing context and can use hardware accelerated OpenGL® function calls to directly display the rendered content.

The CUDA™ rendering modules use an OpenGL® Pixel Buffer Object (PBO) for direct rendering. This is a feature that is provided by CUDA™, which interfaces with OpenGL® or DirectX® via an interoperability layer. The directly rendered result is then retrieved by the CPU by either invoking calls to immediately read pixels to an array in memory, or by accessing it via frame buffer objects and texture read-back. Compositing is then performed by the thread having access to the viewing context, which finally displays the composited image.

When rendering on a cluster, a dedicated server process is started on the nodes. This process maintains a separate instance of the Virvo library and communicates with the display node using an abstract network connection interface. This server process was implemented as a separate tool that ships with DeskVOX. This tool is not limited to being used with the DeskVOX application, but is accessible to any application that uses Virvo for DVR.

5.4   Results

The competitiveness of the many-core DVR implementations was evaluated by performing measurements of the *execution time* as an approximation of their *processor time*. Performance tests were carried out for the various sort-first ray casting implementations. While GPUs and similar coprocessors used for the evaluation are solely dedicated to rendering (or to performing tasks that indirectly serve the rendering task, such as swapping data to and from the cache), CPUs are typically used to perform tasks not related to rendering, such as displaying the GUI of the operating system or performing operating system tasks in general. During the collection of the timing results, care was taken to ensure that no additional, compute intensive tasks compete with the rendering task for CPU resources.

Figure 5.4 depicts the volume datasets that were used to evaluate the performance of the individual implementations. For the measurements, specific post-classification transfer functions were applied to each dataset, which only differ regarding their color mapping. The alpha mapping, if not stated otherwise, was the same for each dataset: a *ramp* that linearly ascends from fully transparent to fully opaque while the density value of the volume sample increases from 0 to 1. Further, local illumination was disabled. The reasoning behind this was to create a most similar basis for the comparison. Local illumination calculations typically are gradient-based and only apply to volumetric regions with a sufficiently high gradient magnitude. Note that in the figure, different color transfer functions as well as local illumination are enabled for aesthetic reasons. The datasets in general vary regarding their spatial extent and the number of time steps they store. While the *engine* dataset, in combination with the specific transfer function applied, exhibits a strong isosurface, which occludes most inner parts of the engine, the *visible male* CT-scan dataset was rendered with a transfer function that reconstructs the bones with full opacity, and the surrounding tissue so that one can see through it to the bones. The *aneurism* dataset is less dense, so that a significant part of the dataset does not contribute to the actually rendered image. In those cases, the early-ray termination optimization will not apply and rays have to be fully traversed through the volume. The large-eddy simulation dataset (*LES*) was the output from a scientific simulation of a weather phenomenon called a

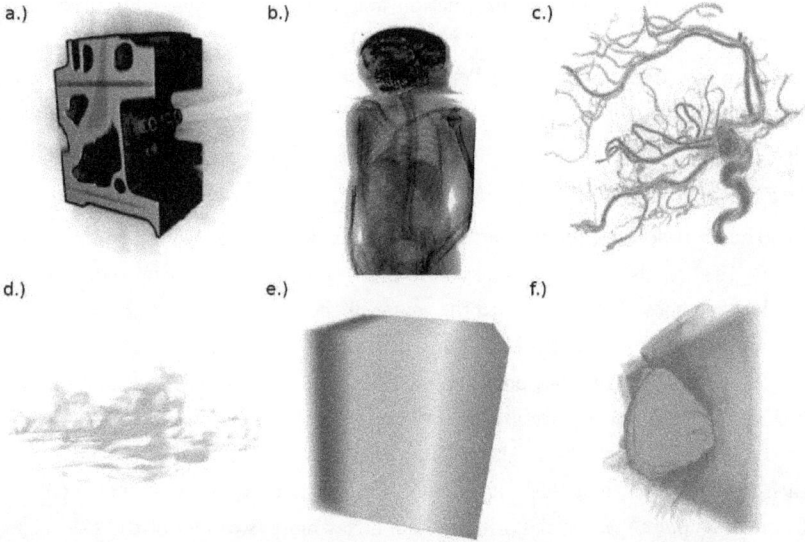

Figure 5.4: Datasets used for the evaluation of the sort-first DVR implementations. From left to right, top to bottom: a.) Engine dataset (256 x 256 x 128 x 1, 1 channel, 8 bit per channel), b.) Visible Human CT-scan (512 x 512 x 1877 x 1, 1 channel, 8 bit per channel), c.) Aneurism (256 x 256 x 256 x 1, 1 channel, 8 bit per channel), d.) Large-eddy simulation (199 x 199 x 89 x 360, 1 channel, 8 bit per channel), e.) Artificial dataset with gradually changing density (32 x 32 x 32 x 1, 1 channel, 8 bit per channel), f.) CT-scan dataset (256 x 256 x 512 x 1, 1 channel, 16 bit per channel).

dustdevil. Only the dust concentration is contained in the volumetric presentation of this dataset. The animation consists of 360 time steps. A more thorough explanation of the simulation and the simulated phenomenon can be found in [KS13]. The transfer function applied to the dataset is not a ramp like it was applied to the other datasets. Instead, it assigns zero opacity to the data items ranging from 0 to approximately 0.1. The transfer function was designed to reveal eddy phenomena around the ground plane and results in a highly transparent dataset. Similar to the aneurism test scenario, this is challenging for the early-ray termination optimization. The *gradient* dataset is an artificial dataset which varies the density gradually along one principal axis. The *carp* dataset, in contrast to the other datasets, stores 16 bit density values at the grid cells.

The timing procedure for the various algorithms was the following. Screen sizes of 1920×1080 pixels (*Full HD*) were considered. An automated test procedure was set up that first moved the volume to the center of the viewing frustum using a *view all* operation (i. e. determine the bounding sphere of the volume and locate the camera at the outer rim of the dataset, pointing towards the center of the dataset). The volume was then rotated in incremental steps about the three principal world coordinate axes. The incremental step size was $2°$, the volume was rotated 90 times about each axis, resulting in a $180°$ rotation and 270 different view points. This procedure favors view points where the primary rays hit at most two sides of the axis-aligned bounding box of the volume. In general, this may lead to a more coherent traversal pattern compared to an arbitrary rotation in 3D space. Although this behavior has probably less influence on these particular tests, the rotations were nevertheless not performed exactly about the principal axes, but a slight, random deviation was introduced. The procedure was carried out *two* times per test modality. To account for potential cache warm-up effects, the first pass was however discarded, so that the actual timing procedure was performed for 270 frames in total. The time to render a single frame was then determined by averaging the total execution time over the 270 rendered frames. All test modalities were configured to use the early-ray termination optimization. Along each ray, opacity was gathered up to a threshold of 95 %, and if this threshold was surpassed, ray traversal was terminated. When rays were traversed in packets, packet traversal was of course only terminated if all rays in the packet had finished traversal. The volumes were sampled with a step width that was inversely proportional to the number of voxels contained in the volumes along one principal axis.

	Engine	Visible Male	Aneurism	LES	Gradient	Carp
Avg. Pixels	25 %	4 %	36 %	21 %	35 %	5 %

Table 5.1: Relative screen space occupied by the various datasets, based on averaging the axis-aligned bounding rectangles in window coordinates over each frame of the timing procedure.

The view all operation to locate the dataset at a distant position implies that only some portions of the screen are actually covered by the volume. Depending on the properties of the datasets, those portions may differ considerably. The *Visible Male* dataset and the *Carp* dataset for instance are narrow, which results in the dataset being moved relatively far away from the viewing position. Less screen space being occupied by the dataset will generally result in a lower rendering workload. Table 5.1 gives an overview of the average portion of screen space that each volume occupied during the rendering procedure, relative to the actually available 1920 × 1080 pixels. The values were obtained by performing the timing procedure once for each dataset and computing the *axis-aligned* bounding rectangle of each view in window coordinates. The bounding rectangle was deduced by projecting the axis-aligned bounding box to window coordinates.

The ensuing evaluation summarizes the timing measurements for the *Array of Structure*-based code path targeted towards CPUs, the *Structure of Array*-based code path that was implemented with SSE, the Intel® Xeon Phi™ code path as well as the code path using NVIDIA® CUDA™. All results presented in this section were obtained by executing the volume rendering application remotely using X11 forwarding. However, only the actual rendering time was measured. More specifically, any setup time for color buffers, or time for copying data to and from a GPU or a coprocessor was omitted. The reasoning behind this is better comparability between the various modes. In principal, it would e. g. be possible to perform direct rendering using pixel buffer objects on a GPU, while this is not an option on the Intel® Xeon Phi™ which is not equipped with a graphics output. Setup times and copying incur constant overhead. Furthermore, changes in technology may very well render the overhead of copying data over PCIe obsolete in the near future. By omitting the communication overhead from the results, their significance will then, however, stay the same.

	1 Thread	2 Threads	4 Threads	8 Threads	16 Threads
Engine	**1.015**	**0.510**	**0.258**	**0.131**	0.067
Visible Male	**0.239**	**0.121**	**0.064**	**0.034**	0.017
Aneurism	**2.872**	**1.439**	**0.723**	**0.364**	0.183
LES	**0.682**	**0.345**	**0.175**	**0.090**	0.047
Gradient	**0.471**	**0.239**	**0.123**	**0.065**	0.034
Carp	**0.149**	**0.077**	0.041	0.023	0.013

Table 5.2: Average rendering times in seconds using the AoS-based CPU renderer and nearest neighbor reconstruction.

	1 Thread	2 Threads	4 Threads	8 Threads	16 Threads
Engine	**1.954**	**0.984**	**0.493**	**0.249**	0.126
Visible Male	**0.483**	**0.247**	**0.127**	**0.067**	0.032
Aneurism	**5.658**	**2.833**	**1.421**	**0.712**	0.357
LES	**1.297**	**0.646**	**0.326**	**0.166**	0.085
Gradient	**0.820**	**0.412**	**0.210**	**0.108**	0.056
Carp	**0.261**	**0.133**	0.069	0.037	0.020

Table 5.3: Average rendering times in seconds using the AoS-based CPU renderer and trilinear interpolation.

Tables 5.2, 5.3, 5.4, and 5.5 summarize the timing results for the sort-first ray casting implementation targeted towards CPUs. All measurements were performed on a system with two Intel® Xeon® E5-2690 octa-core server CPUs. Each physical core has a maximal clock rate of 2.90 GHz. Intel®'s hyper-threading technology [Per05] was deactivated, so that 16 cores could be used concurrently. All executables were created using the Intel® Compiler, version 14.0.1, and the compiler option -O2 for optimization. Threads were *"pinned"* so that exactly one thread was scheduled per core. The tables show results for tests using AoS-based rendering with nearest neighbor reconstruction, AoS-based rendering with trilinear interpolation, SoA-

	1 Thread	2 Threads	4 Threads	8 Threads	16 Threads
Engine	**0.302**	**0.155**	**0.080**	0.042	0.023
Visible Male	0.083	0.044	0.024	0.015	0.008
Aneurism	**0.878**	0.442	0.224	0.114	0.059
LES	**0.198**	**0.103**	0.054	0.030	0.016
Gradient	**0.121**	**0.063**	0.035	0.021	0.011
Carp	0.054	0.029	0.017	0.011	0.006

Table 5.4: Average rendering times in seconds using the SoA-based SSE renderer and nearest neighbor reconstruction.

	1 Thread	2 Threads	4 Threads	8 Threads	16 Threads
Engine	**0.409**	**0.207**	**0.106**	**0.055**	0.029
Visible Male	0.112	0.059	0.033	0.020	0.011
Aneurism	**1.175**	**0.590**	**0.297**	**0.151**	**0.076**
LES	**0.259**	**0.132**	0.069	0.037	**0.020**
Gradient	**0.155**	**0.081**	0.044	0.025	0.013
Carp	0.062	0.034	0.019	0.012	0.007

Table 5.5: Average rendering times in seconds using the SoA-based SSE renderer and trilinear interpolation.

based rendering with nearest neighbor reconstruction, and SoA-based rendering with trilinear interpolation, respectively.

Among other factors, the scaling behavior of the ray casting implementation is of interest. Therefore, the CPU implementations were evaluated by performing measurements using 1, 2, 4, 8, or 16 concurrent CPU threads. Table 5.6 and 5.7 deduce the *parallel efficiency* (speedup over processor count) from the raw data tables for the SoA implementation and the two reconstruction modes. To calculate the speedup (cf. Equation 3.29), the portions of the serial code that is executed and the portions of the code that execute in parallel must be known. For lack of this information, the speedup is approximated as the time it takes a single thread to render an image over the time it takes N threads to render the same image. Figure 5.7 and 5.8 also show plots of the efficiency. In general, all scenarios in any case exhibit good scalability up to the maximum of 16 threads. The use of SoA packets

	1 Thread	2 Threads	4 Threads	8 Threads	16 Threads
Engine	1.000	0.974	0.944	0.899	0.821
Visible Male	1.000	0.943	0.865	0.692	0.648
Aneurism	1.000	0.993	0.980	0.963	0.930
LES	1.000	0.961	0.917	0.825	0.773
Gradient	1.000	0.960	0.864	0.720	0.688
Carp	1.000	0.931	0.794	0.614	0.563

Table 5.6: Parallel efficiency of the SoA-based SSE renderer with nearest neighbor reconstruction (see also Figure 5.7).

	1 Thread	2 Threads	4 Threads	8 Threads	16 Threads
Engine	1.000	0.988	0.965	0.930	0.881
Visible Male	1.000	0.949	0.848	0.700	0.636
Aneurism	1.000	0.996	0.989	0.973	0.966
LES	1.000	0.981	0.938	0.875	0.809
Gradient	1.000	0.957	0.881	0.775	0.745
Carp	1.000	0.912	0.816	0.646	0.554

Table 5.7: Parallel efficiency of the SoA-based SSE renderer with trilinear interpolation (see also Figure 5.8).

compared to single-ray traversal leads to nearly linear scaling, too. The differences range from factor 3 up to a factor of nearly 5 for the scenario with the Aneurism dataset and linear interpolation, even though packets of size 4 suggest a maximum acceleration of factor 4. The sub-linear speedup can be explained by cache coherence. Ray packets can make better use of caches because coherent primary rays, as they are used when evaluating the absorption and emission model, tend to access adjacent memory regions. With single-ray traversal, the rays handling one tile are traversed consecutively using a depth-first pattern, so that adjacent rays cannot benefit from cache coherence.

Another interesting aspect is the influence of memory accesses on performance. Performing trilinear interpolation in order to reconstruct the volume dataset at a sample position requires *eight* memory accesses, while assigning the value of the nearest voxel requires only *one* memory access. All tests were thus performed

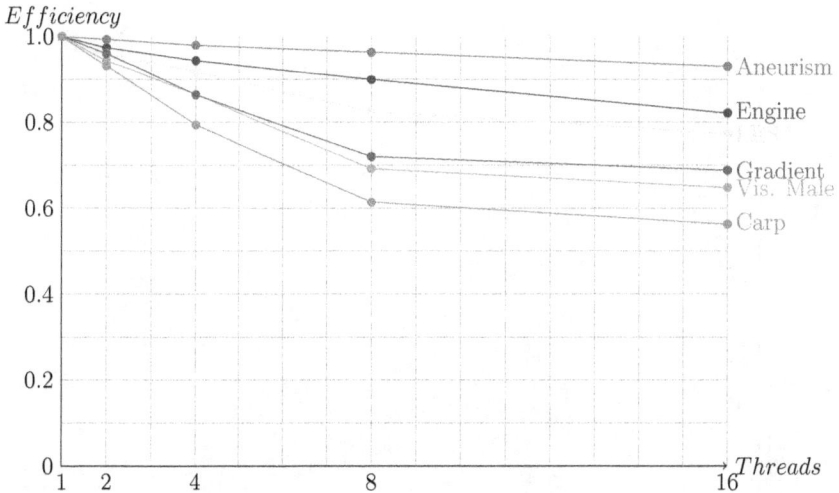

Figure 5.5: Parallel efficiency of the SoA-based SSE renderer with nearest neighbor reconstruction (see also Table 5.6).

both for reconstruction using the nearest neighbor method as well as for trilinear interpolation. Note that on GPUs, trilinear interpolation can be performed in hardware and the CUDA™ implementation makes use of this fact. The results obtained from evaluating the CPU implementations show some interesting behavior in this regard. Rendering with AoS and trilinear interpolation takes about twice the time it takes to render with AoS and the nearest neighbor method, although eight times more memory accesses are necessary. This is due to the fact that the data items used for interpolation are typically adjacent and thus likely to already be in the cache. With the ray packet implementation, however, the overhead for trilinear interpolation is only proportional to a factor of 1.5, and even lower factors in certain cases, which supports the assumption that SoA traversal results in memory access patterns that yield a better cache utilization.

Table 5.8 and 5.9 summarize the results for the Xeon Phi™ code path for nearest neighbor reconstruction and trilinear interpolation, respectively. Table 5.10 and 5.11 show the parallel efficiency deduced from Table 5.8 and 5.9 for 30, 45, 60, 120,

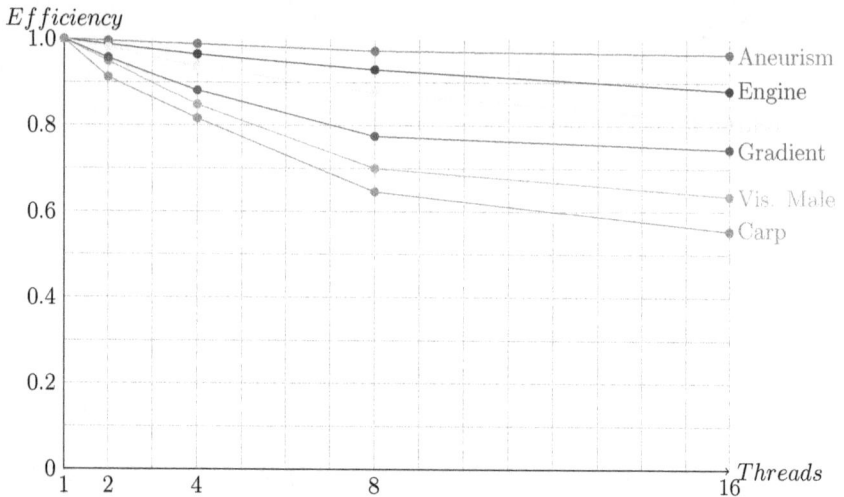

Figure 5.6:   Parallel efficiency of the SoA-based SSE renderer with trilinear interpolation (see also Table 5.7).

and 240 Threads, respectively. The executable was also compiled with the Intel® compiler, version 14.0.1, and the compiler flag -O2 for optimization. For the tests, the threads were *"pinned"* in order to prohibit rescheduling on another core. Above the limit of 120 threads, i. e. when two threads were scheduled per core, the scalability in general dropped. Nevertheless, for datasets imposing a high workload, like the *Aneurism* dataset, scheduling up to four threads per core results in a performance increase. It is notable that the algorithm, though being embarrassingly parallel in theory, does not scale *linearly* up to 120 threads and above. However, the flattening of the scalability curve can have various reasons. In general, devising schemes to balance the workload among the threads even better would probably be worth the effort. On the other hand, the drop in scalability could very well be due to contention, because 240 threads simultaneously access the memory controller of the coprocessor. A reason like that could probably only be mitigated by a complete algorithmic redesign. Nevertheless, because the coprocessor code path in general is competitive and the algorithm itself is embarrassingly parallel and thus very well suited for the MIC architecture, such an effort could lead to unforeseen issues which might impact

	1 Thrd.	30 Thrd.	45 Thrd.	60 Thrd.	120 Thrd.	240 Thrd.
Engine	0.744	0.045	0.027	0.022	0.015	0.014
Visible Male	0.361	0.017	0.013	0.011	0.009	0.010
Aneurism	2.241	0.107	0.074	0.059	0.033	0.028
LES	0.327	0.022	0.017	0.014	0.010	0.010
Gradient	0.207	0.017	0.012	0.011	0.011	0.014
Carp	0.223	0.012	0.008	0.007	0.006	0.006

Table 5.8: Average rendering times in seconds using the Xeon Phi^{TM} renderer and nearest neighbor reconstruction.

	1 Thrd.	30 Thrd.	45 Thrd.	60 Thrd.	120 Thrd.	240 Thrd.
Engine	1.629	0.071	0.049	0.042	0.024	0.025
Visible Male	1.170	0.050	0.036	0.032	0.022	0.021
Aneurism	4.997	0.200	0.136	0.102	0.058	0.046
LES	0.484	0.032	0.022	0.019	0.012	0.011
Gradient	0.281	0.025	0.016	0.018	0.014	0.017
Carp	0.526	0.024	0.018	0.014	0.011	0.012

Table 5.9: Average rendering times in seconds using the Xeon Phi^{TM} renderer and trilinear interpolation.

performance. The efficiency comparison also suggests that the higher the workload, the better the scalability. For instance, the efficiency in general increases when linear interpolation is performed instead of nearest neighbor reconstruction.

A special trait of the Intel® Xeon Phi^{TM} coprocessor is the existence of dedicated instructions for gathering data from an array using incoherent integer indices. Table 5.12 compares the code path where the volume texture lookup routine and the transfer function lookup routine were optimized using a total of five gather instructions, and a code path where this behavior was emulated by copying the indices to general-purpose registers and constructing new SIMD vectors following the table lookups. The ray casting algorithm performs these two types of lookups in its innermost loop, and optimizing them is crucial to obtain maximum performance. In the case of trilinear interpolation, volume lookup happens eight times, while the lookup to the RGBA transfer function is carried out only once. The differences in performance for the two

	1 Thrd.	30 Thrd.	45 Thrd.	60 Thrd.	120 Thrd.	240 Thrd.
Engine	1.000	0.551	0.612	0.564	0.413	0.221
Visible Male	1.000	0.708	0.617	0.547	0.334	0.150
Aneurism	1.000	0.698	0.673	0.633	0.566	0.333
LES	1.000	0.495	0.427	0.389	0.273	0.136
Gradient	1.000	0.406	0.383	0.314	0.157	0.062
Carp	1.000	0.619	0.619	0.531	0.310	0.155

Table 5.10:   Parallel efficiency of the Xeon Phi^{TM} implementation with nearest neighbor reconstruction (see also Table 5.10).

	1 Thrd.	30 Thrd.	45 Thrd.	60 Thrd.	120 Thrd.	240 Thrd.
Engine	1.000	0.765	0.738	0.646	0.566	0.272
Visible Male	1.000	0.780	0.722	0.610	0.443	0.232
Aneurism	1.000	0.833	0.817	0.817	0.718	0.453
LES	1.000	0.504	0.489	0.425	0.336	0.183
Gradient	1.000	0.375	0.390	0.260	0.167	0.068
Carp	1.000	0.731	0.649	0.626	0.399	0.183

Table 5.11:   Parallel efficiency of the Xeon Phi^{TM} implementation with trilinear interpolation. (see also Table 5.11).

code paths were striking, anyway. For the compute intensive *Aneurism* and *LES* datasets and reconstruction using trilinear interpolation, for instance, performance more than doubled when the gather intrinsics were used. The increase in performance when rendering the other datasets in general was significant, specifically if trilinear interpolation was used and the copying of indices to general-purpose registers occurred eight times. These two functionalities, volume lookup and transfer function lookup, are at the heart of any DVR algorithm, so that it is crucial to apply this optimization when implementing DVR on the MIC architecture in general. The author of this thesis wonders, why the auto-vectorizer was not able to recognize this distinct memory access pattern and perform this optimization automatically.

The GPGPU used for the evaluation of the CUDA^{TM} ray casting implementation is an NVIDIA® Tesla® K20^{TM} . The Tesla® series is targeted towards the compute segment and does, like the Intel® coprocessor, not have a graphics output. Because

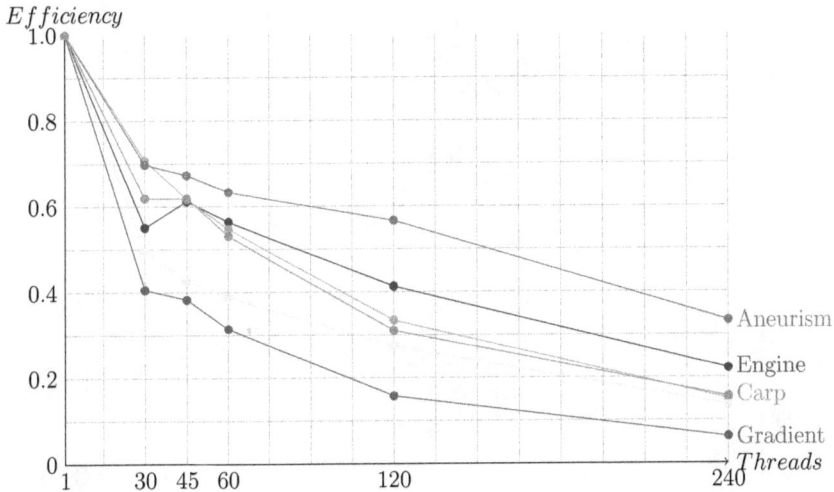

Figure 5.7: Parallel efficiency of the Xeon Phi™ implementation with nearest neighbor reconstruction (see also Table 5.10).

of that, the GPGPU is also operated using remote rendering. However, like this was the case for the other implementations, only the actual rendering phase of the ray casting algorithm was measured and overhead for copying data to and from the device are omitted from the results. Tables 5.13 and 5.14 present the rendering times using CUDA™ , and additionally summarize the results of all the other implementations for comparison. For brevity's sake, a scalability analysis of the ray casting algorithm is omitted for the CUDA™ code path.

At first sight, one can see from the results that trilinear interpolation is virtually free on GPGPUs, while the optimized x86 code paths impose an increase of factor 1.5 for first-order reconstruction. The GPGPU implementation in general outperforms both x86 implementations. The Intel® Xeon Phi™ implementation is superior to the CPU implementation regarding rendering times, specifically if the dataset imposes a relatively high workload.

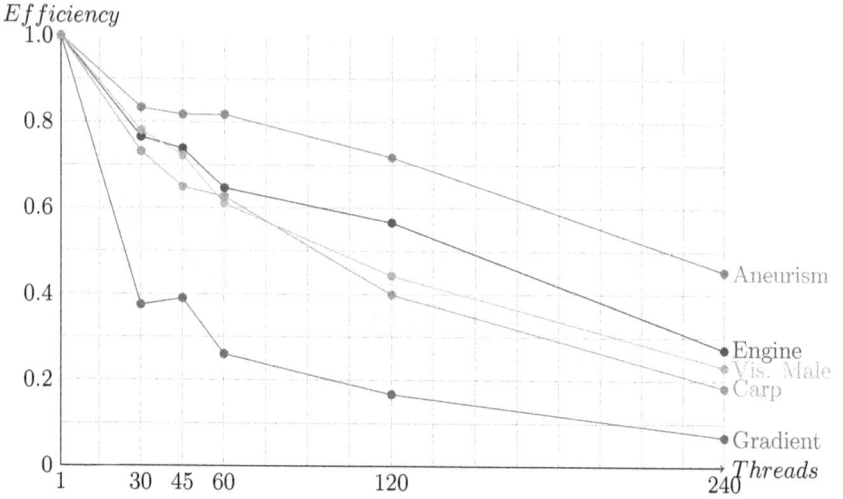

Figure 5.8: Parallel efficiency of the Xeon Phi™ implementation with trilinear interpolation (see also Table 5.11).

	no gather, nn	gather, nn	no gather, lerp	gather, lerp
Engine	0.016	0.014	0.035	0.025
Visible Male	0.010	0.010	0.024	0.021
Aneurism	0.036	0.028	0.114	0.046
LES	0.012	0.010	0.024	0.011
Gradient	0.016	0.014	0.028	0.017
Carp	0.007	0.006	0.014	0.012

Table 5.12: Average rendering times in seconds on the Intel® Xeon Phi™ . Columns from left to right: 1.) without gather optimization and with nearest neighbor reconstruction, 2.) with gather optimization and with nearest neighbor reconstruction, 3.) without gather optimization and with trilinear interpolation, 4.) with gather optimization and with trilinear interpolation. All results were obtained on the Xeon Phi™ coprocessor using 240 threads.

	AoS CPU	SoA CPU	MIC	CUDA
Engine	0.067	0.023	0.014	0.011
Visible Male	0.017	0.008	0.009	0.007
Aneurism	0.183	0.059	0.028	0.016
LES	0.047	0.016	0.010	0.008
Gradient	0.034	0.011	0.011	0.008
Carp	0.013	0.006	0.006	0.006

Table 5.13: Average rendering times in seconds for all four code paths and nearest neighbor reconstruction.

	AoS CPU	SoA CPU	MIC	CUDA
Engine	0.126	0.029	0.024	0.011
Visible Male	0.032	0.011	0.021	0.007
Aneurism	0.357	0.076	0.046	0.017
LES	0.085	0.020	0.011	0.008
Gradient	0.056	0.013	0.014	0.008
Carp	0.020	0.007	0.011	0.006

Table 5.14: Average rendering times in seconds for all four code paths and trilinear interpolation.

5.5   Conclusions

This section investigated implementation issues for porting DVR ray casting to heterogeneous HPC platforms. In a most theoretical sense, the problem of marching individual rays through a volume density must be considered embarrassingly parallel. Unfortunately, because of the memory bottleneck of contemporary computers, and the fact that volume ray casting is especially memory bound, actual implementations must find a way to align memory access patterns that reduce cache misses. This section proposed several implementations that target several HPC platforms, which are not necessarily a good match for DVR. The section showed that the ray casting algorithm as a popular representative of DVR algorithms in general can be implemented to be competitive when compared to a GPGPU implementation. GPGPUs are naturally a good match for DVR algorithms, which benefit from high throughput and hardware support for trilinear interpolation.

Intel® x86-compatible CPUs expose parallelism through a shared memory architecture that can be programmed in a Multiple Instruction, Multiple Data (MIMD) fashion, and through SIMD registers with special vector instructions. It was shown that for ordinary ray marching with coherent memory access patterns, ray packet traversal using a *Structure of Arrays* layout is superior over single-ray traversal. These findings match the observations that were previously made by other researchers regarding surface ray tracing. Traversing rays in packets imposes an extra amount of complexity on software design. The section devised wrapper structures with which it is possible to write packet traversal as if a single ray was traversed. The results show that mimicking single-ray traversal by using wrapper classes for SIMD vector data types can result in efficient code being generated by the compiler, if the function and data structure layout allows all constructs to be inlined by the compiler, and if additional overhead like that for template instantiation is resolved at compile time. The results also show that programming on the instruction level with intrinsics is beneficial. This was especially true for the implementation targeting the Intel® Xeon Phi™ coprocessor, which provides special intrinsics for incoherent memory accesses from a linear array. Here, the compiler would not make use of these special instructions on its own, and thus explicit use of vector instructions was necessary to fully exploit the capabilities of the coprocessor's instruction set architecture. The Intel® Xeon Phi™ code path is especially interesting because it demonstrates that the ray casting algorithm is able to scale up to hundreds of concurrent threads. Nevertheless, it was impossible to outperform CPU ray casting by orders of magnitude. In general, the *efficiency* of the coprocessor implementation increases with higher workloads. On x86-compatible architectures, when using packet ray traversal, the costs for first-order reconstruction, which implies accessing the eight surrounding voxels of the sampling position, amounts to approximately 1.5 times the costs for nearest neighbor reconstruction, which requires only a single voxel lookup.

Compared to x86 architectures, GPGPUs have an advantage because they provide highly optimized and hardwired memory access mechanisms for 3D arrays. Because of that, first-order texture reconstruction comes at virtually no additional cost compared to nearest neighbor reconstruction. On top of that, GPGPUs nowadays provide a highly flexible programming model based on multiple threads that act like being linked in a SIMD fashion, but that can be programmed largely without communication among each other. On the downside, using GPGPUs imposes the additional overhead of having to communicate via PCIe, which is impractical especially if dataset sizes exceed the amount of video memory available on the GPU.

Chapter 6

Decoupling Rendering and Display Phase

A special trait of the Distributed Volume Rendering Pipeline outlined in Section 4.2 is the display phase that follows after image generation and compositing. Logically decoupling the display phase from the prior stages has the advantage that it can be specialized in a variety of different ways. This section proposes to decouple the display phase from rendering to hide latency that is inflicted upon the whole Distributed Rendering Pipeline. The technique described in this section is an approximate method targeted towards interactive applications like visualization in Virtual Reality, where frame rates that drop significantly below 30 Hz can cause fatigue or even nausea.

This chapter is in parts based upon a conference publication by Zellmann et al. [ZAL12] and is structured as follows. Section 6.1 gives an introduction to remote rendering as well as image-based rendering and provides a brief overview of work that relates to the method proposed by this work. Then, in Section 6.2 an image-based remote rendering technique is presented that employs image reprojection, which decouples the rendering stage from the display stage, and which is thus capable of hiding latency. Sections 6.3 and 6.4 propose several enhancements to the image-based remote rendering technique and how it can be integrated with interactive applications. Section 6.5 presents results from a formal evaluation of the proposed algorithm, while

Section 6.6 briefly concludes this chapter.

6.1   Image-Based Remote Volume Rendering

Remote rendering is a technique where rendering workloads are physically decoupled for load balancing purposes. Typically, the rendering task is subdivided into compute intensive and less compute intensive tasks, which are then distributed among a pool of compute resources that are usually spatially detached. In the case of DVR, the compute intensive parts comprise volume integration and image compositing, while displaying the final image is considered a cheap operation. Specific implementations usually realize remote rendering over commodity networks using the TCP/IP protocol layer or low-latency networks like InfiniBand® [Pfi01]. Implementations are then usually based on a client-server model.

When applied to the Distributed Volume Rendering Pipeline, the rendering phase and the compositing phase are assigned to one remote computer or a network of remote computers, while the display phase is assigned to the client computer. While the subdivision into phases which are distributed among a pool of compute resources could in general be accomplished in different ways, for the purposes of this section the term remote rendering will be referred to as described above. The server-side of the remote rendering application is responsible for rendering and compositing, while the client-side is responsible to display the final image.

The client that is responsible for the display phase is often equipped with less capable rendering hardware than the computer or the network of computers assigned to the rendering and compositing phase. Because this is not only true for remote rendering applied to DVR, but also for other scenarios, the display computer for remote rendering is often portable or even a handheld device. A broad overview of remote rendering in general can be found in the PhD thesis of Dieter Schmalstieg [Sch97].

Remote rendering can be implemented into the renderer module of a visualization application or as a middleware that the visualization software uses to transfer control information and rendered images. Examples of such a middleware are the remote display capabilities of the X Window System [LWK05], the VNC remote desktop application [RSFWH98] or the dedicated remote rendering software VirtualGL [Com14b].

Stegmaier et al. [SME02] presented a general remote rendering middleware that uses the X Window remote display functionality, but directly intercepts the graphics API calls for rendering by replacing the GLX library of the operating system with a customized one. The replacement library renders images into a GLX Pbuffer off-screen render target. When the GLX call was issued that swaps the back buffer and the front buffer, instead of being displayed, the Pbuffer's content is downloaded to main memory and then transferred over the network to the client-side for display.

In contrast to that, Sharp et al. [SRC10] developed a specialized remote rendering system that is dedicated to remote volume rendering in clinical environments. Their solution is coupled with CT scanning devices and can produce interactive images on the fly. The system supports a multi-user environment. The target platform is a Multi-GPU cluster environment that delivers remote rendered images to thin clients used by physicians in the operating rooms.

The highest degree of specialization is achievable if the remote rendering software is integrated into the visualization application. That way, certain assumptions about the rendered data can be made that would be invalid in general. Only hardware accelerated algorithms can benefit from specialized middleware like VirtualGL or the approach proposed by Stegmaier et al. Mere X Window remote display is a general solution to the remote rendering problem, but is inefficient in the context of hardware accelerated rendering because graphics API calls are not directly processed but sent to the client-side, where they are executed. This behavior results in high bandwidth requirements and the necessity of the client computer to be equipped with dedicated graphics hardware.

Pajak et al. [PHE+11] proposed an algorithm where low-resolution images are rendered using a deferred-shading like algorithm on the server, which is then send to the client along with depth information and motion flow images. From these, the client can then reconstruct a lossy, high-resolution image. Because of the low resolution of the images processed on the server, the authors' subdivision into stages differed from the traditional remote rendering pipeline, because a significant amount of work is transferred from the server-side to the client-side. The publication also focused on compression suitable for the depth images and the motion-flow images and in that way relates to the technique proposed in this thesis, which also relies on transferring depth images over a network connection.

Image-based rendering (IBR) aims at the reconstruction of the plenoptic function of a 3D environment based on discrete samples. IBR techniques traditionally originated from efforts to approximate photorealistic image synthesis by directly altering real images or images that were already synthesized, but e. g. for an alternative camera transformation. IBR techniques can be classified based upon the extent to which an explicit geometry is necessary to synthesize the image. A classification of different IBR techniques was given by Shum and Kang [SK00]. A more comprehensive introduction to image-based rendering can e. g. be found in the textbook by Shum et al. [SCK11].

Shade et al. [SGHS98] proposed the layered depth image (LDI) approach, which in terms of the classification from Shum and Kang falls in the category of IBR techniques with an explicit geometry. In addition to the color information, a depth information is stored along with each pixel. The images are stored in multiple layers with different depths and then warped according to the current camera transform. Because the depth images overlap, disocclusion artifacts that occur when 2D images are warped are no longer visible. If the view point differs significantly from the view point the LDI was generated for, holes between the layers become visible.

Coconu's and Hege's publication [CH02] relates to the work in this thesis because they also used an image-based technique using hardware accelerated point cloud rendering. They implemented a level-of-detail approach by organizing a 3D scene using an octree data structure. Depending on the level-of-detail, surfaces are either represented as triangles or as points. They also had to face occurrences of holes in-between the point cloud and met the resulting artifacts by expanding the points to elliptical splats.

6.2 Remote Rendering Technique

This work exploits remote rendering in conjunction with an IBR technique to decouple rendering and the ensuing display phase to hide latency. The IBR technique falls in the category of algorithms with an explicit geometry. The remote rendering algorithm is implemented as part of the visualization software DeskVOX and is specifically designed to be used with DVR.

In the following, the computers that are used to perform rendering and compositing are holistically referred to as the server, while the computer responsible for the display phase will be called the client. The following subsections elaborate on the various steps that are performed on both the server-side and the client-side.

6.2.1 Remote Rendering of 2.5D Image Data to Hide Latency

Remote rendering scenarios are subject to latency from several sources. Delays are not only due to the possibility of excessive rendering times, but also due to the added communication overhead that arises when having to transfer image data over a network connection. The technique proposed by this work aims at hiding that latency by decoupling the display stage from the prior stages of the Distributed Volume Rendering Pipeline.

The display phase of the Distributed Volume Rendering Pipeline is executed on the client-side. Other than with ordinary remote rendering approaches, the technique proposed by this work relies on image data that is accompanied by a depth buffer that is generated on the server and then sent to the client for display. That way, the server is not required to send data to the client at a refresh rate of 30 Hz. Rather than that, the 2.5D dataset can be used to generate an approximate image that is visually plausible, which is the case if the current view point and the view point the 2.5D dataset was generated for differ only slightly.

The client initially creates two threads for image data retrieval and asynchronous rendering, respectively (cf. Figure 6.1). The first thread maintains a socket connec-

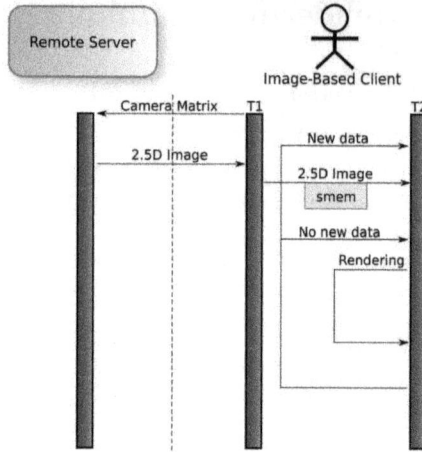

Figure 6.1: The image-based client application maintains two threads to asynchronously render the data from the previous frame in one thread and, in the meantime, to listen for view point changes and new data in the second thread.

tion, which is used to send the camera transformation to the server, whenever the camera view point is changed. Then the thread listens for new 2.5D data sent back by the server. When 2.5D image data is obtained from the server, the dataset is stored to a memory location shared by the two threads.

The second thread is responsible for asynchronously rendering the 2.5D dataset. This is done by transforming the 2.5D image buffer to 3D point primitives that can be displayed using GPU hardware acceleration. Initially and whenever the size of the viewport of the viewing window is changed, a new vertex buffer object (VBO) is created to contain the points. The world space x- and y-positions of the points depend on the image space coordinates of their associated image pixels and are thus constant. The z-coordinates that depend on the depth buffer sent along with the image data on the other hand changes from frame to frame. Recreating the whole VBO for each new frame was found to be too time consuming by Zellmann et al. and led to a palpable interruption when new data was received. To avoid this interruption, VBOs are only recreated initially and on changing the viewport of the viewing window. As long as the viewport stays the same, the x- and y-positions of the points do not need to be updated because their assignment to image pixels does not change. What does change is the z-position of the points, which depends on the newly created depth buffer that is sent along with the image data, as well as the image data itself. Therefore, for interactive updates, a vertex shader is used that processes all incoming point primitives and adjusts their position based on a texture lookup. The new depth values are sent to the vertex stage using a 2D texture. The same is done for the color values, which are sent to the vertex shader using an uncompressed RGBA texture. The vertex shader adjusts only the z-positions of the points and their associated colors. As far as the viewport does not change, but new 2.5D is received from the server, only the textures need to be updated, which is a lightweight operation compared to recreating the whole VBO.

6.2.2 Constructing the Reprojection Matrix

Instead of merely applying the actual camera transform for the current camera configuration to the vertices, the vertex shader is also used to perform the reprojection step by applying the associated reprojection matrix to all points in parallel. This matrix is constructed on the client-side based on the camera transform which was valid when the 2.5D dataset was created. The old camera transform is retrieved from the server along with each new dataset. The following subsection describes the construction of the reprojection matrix.

In order to reduce bandwidth pressure, the remote rendering technique relies on storing the depth buffer with one byte per sample. Thus, so that no precision is unnecessarily lost, in the case of this technique, image space z-coordinates do not cover the whole range from the near-clipping plane to the far-clipping plane. Only the range that is actually spanned by the volume dataset is stored in the depth buffer. This limited range can then be stored using a higher precision. This strategy is illustrated in Figure 6.2.

The server, when it performs DVR, initially generates sample positions in world space, which are then transformed to image space according to the rules imposed by the rasterization pipeline implemented on current GPUs. In addition to the 2.5D

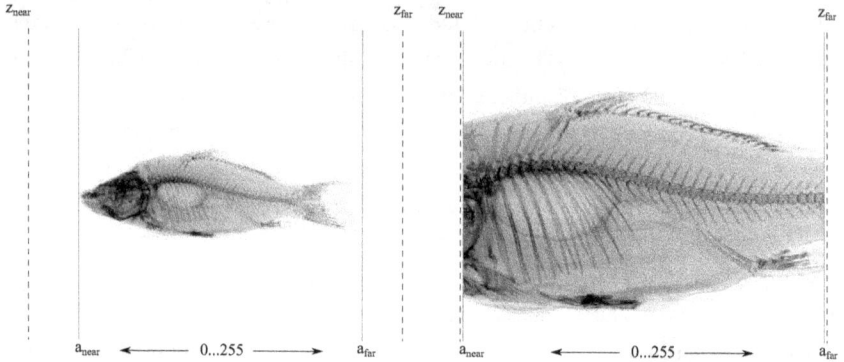

Figure 6.2: Saving depth buffer precision by only storing the limited range spanned by the volumetric region. The left image shows a setup which can benefit from the depth range adjustment by ignoring the empty space beyond a_{near} and a_{far}. The right image is a zoomed in view, where the depth range adjustment is not beneficial because a_{near} coincides with the near-clipping plane and a_{far} coincides with the far-clipping plane.

data samples, the server also records the current camera transform as well as the range that the z-coordinates of the image space samples span to implement the range downscaling technique from above. Neglecting the depth range downscaling, the reprojection method proposed in this work would basically only apply the backwards transform of the camera transform for the original view point to the 2.5D image data and depth buffer. This would result in the points being transformed back to world space. Then the current camera transform could be applied to the world space coordinates by the vertex shader, which would *warp* the 2.5D dataset for the original view point to match the current view point.

The range downscaling requires an additional step during the construction of the reprojection matrix. The reprojection matrix, which is assembled on the client-side, is itself composed of several transforms.

First of all, the image space samples are transformed back to normalized device coordinates. This is done by applying the inverse viewport transform

$$V^{-1} = \begin{pmatrix} \frac{1}{w/2} & 0 & 0 & \frac{l}{w/2} - 1 \\ 0 & \frac{1}{h/2} & 0 & \frac{b}{h/2} - 1 \\ 0 & 0 & 2 & -1 \\ 0 & 0 & 0 & 1 \end{pmatrix} \quad (6.1)$$

to the 2.5D image data, where w and h are the width and height and l and b are the leftmost and bottommost positions of the viewport, respectively.

The points in normalized device coordinates obtained by applying V^{-1} do not yet reflect the adjusted depth range. The depth range that was recorded during rendering is represented by the real numbers a_{near} and a_{far}

with

$$a_{near} \geq z_{near}$$

and

$$a_{far} \leq z_{far}$$

where z_{near} and z_{far} are the near- and the far-clipping plane in normalized device coordinates. The inverse depth range transform is applied by multiplying the matrix

$$D^{-1} = \begin{pmatrix} 1 & 0 & 0 & 0 \\ 0 & 1 & 0 & 0 \\ 0 & 0 & a_{far} - a_{near} & a_{near} \\ 0 & 0 & 0 & 1 \end{pmatrix} \quad (6.2)$$

to the points in normalized device coordinates. These can then be transformed back to world space by application of the ordinary inverse model-view-projection transform, i. e. by first multiplying by the inverse projection matrix PR^{-1} and then by the inverse of the combined model- and view matrix MV^{-1}. The assembled reprojection matrix for warping thus reads

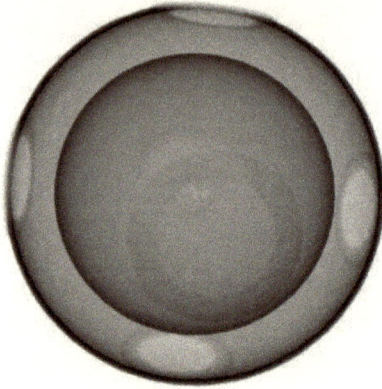

Figure 6.3: Dataset exhibiting multiple layers of translucent media. The transfer function exposes three solid, nested spheres, so that a ray traveling through the medium potentially crosses six boundary layers. A depth value for such a ray is non-obvious.

$$W = MV^{-1} \times PR^{-1} \times D^{-1} \times V^{-1} \qquad (6.3)$$

and is passed to the vertex shader to reproject all 2.5D image points in parallel. The vertex stage of the client program for this simple configuration only consists of applying the reprojection matrix to all vertices.

6.2.3   Depth Buffer Generation from Volumes

The remote rendering technique described in this thesis is in principle not limited to DVR, but is applicable to any rendering algorithm that is able to produce 2.5D image data. Generating a depth buffer from volumes rendered using DVR is however more challenging than e. g. deducing depths from polygonal renderings where no transparency is involved. In the latter case, depending on the rendering algorithm, depth values are easily deduced by using e. g. the first hit position of a primary ray with the scene objects, or the frontmost entry in a z-buffer.

In the case of surface rendering, the depth buffer is easy to deduce because only the cross section between two different media is considered for rendering. In DVR, all participating media contribute to the image. Unlike it is the case with mere surface rendering, volumes are well defined throughout their whole region, and not only at their boundaries. In general, there is not necessarily a distinct cross section between two media along the path of a ray intersecting a volume, and even if there is, contention may arise if more than two different types of medium are intersected by the ray and all of them are assigned translucent colors (cf. Figure 6.3). On top of that, it is not even true that the most plausible depth buffer value for the ray necessarily coincides with one of the boundary layers between participating media. Such a justification is not valid because of the very fact that the volume is well defined at every voxel. Because of this ambiguity, depth buffer generation can only be performed heuristically. Different heuristics may apply based upon certain assumptions. One valid assumption may for instance be that the transfer function extracts an isosurface from the volume data and that all features beyond the isosurface are mostly occluded.

The evaluation of the heuristics described in the remainder of this subsection are based on different assumptions regarding the nature of the transfer function and the volume dataset. They are exemplarily described based on the ray casting algorithm. Anyway, the heuristics are in general applicable to any DVR algorithm but lend themselves well to a ray casting implementation because they rely on the analysis of cumulative quantities that are gathered along single rays.

Heuristics for depth buffer generation are divided into two classes. *Single-pass heuristics* are evaluated during ray traversal. Since no additional rendering pass is necessary, these heuristics are cheap regarding execution time. Conversely, *two-pass heuristics* are evaluated using two rendering passes. These heuristics are expected to produce results of higher quality at the cost of a higher execution time.

The single-pass heuristics comprise the following:

Entry A ray is traversed through the volume once. The depth value is recorded at the z-position where the first non-transparent voxel along the ray was encountered.

Exit A ray is traversed through the volume once. The depth value is recorded at the z-position where the last non-transparent voxel along the ray was encountered.

Midpoint The *Entry* and *Exit* z-positions are recorded in a ray traversal pass. The depth value is recorded at the midpoint between *Entry-* and *Exit* position.

Peak A ray is traversed through the volume once. The depth value is recorded at the z-position where the highest opacity was encountered.

Threshold A ray is traversed through the volume once, and alpha compositing is performed. The depth value is recorded where the accumulated opacity reaches a certain threshold.

Gradient A ray is traversed through the volume once. The depth value is recorded at the z-position with the highest gradient between two neighboring voxels.

The evaluated two-pass heuristics are the following:

Relative Threshold In a first rendering pass, alpha compositing is performed to gather the total opacity encountered along the path of the ray. In a second rendering pass, alpha compositing is performed again and the depth value reaches a certain threshold, that is weighed by the total opacity gathered during the first rendering pass.

Entry / Exit Mean In a first rendering pass the *Entry-* and *Exit* heuristics are evaluated. Then a second ray is traversed and alpha compositing is performed. The depth value is recorded at the z-position where the accumulated opacity reaches the arithmetic mean between *Entry-* and *Exit* opacity.

Note that the *Threshold* single-pass heuristic can only produce useful results for meaningful opacity thresholds. If the threshold cannot be reached along any ray, because the general alpha contribution along the ray is too low, the recorded depth values will coincide with the backsides of the volume's bounding box. Although this problem is less imminent with the *Relative Threshold* heuristic because the threshold is weighed by the total opacity observed along the ray, the opacity threshold should

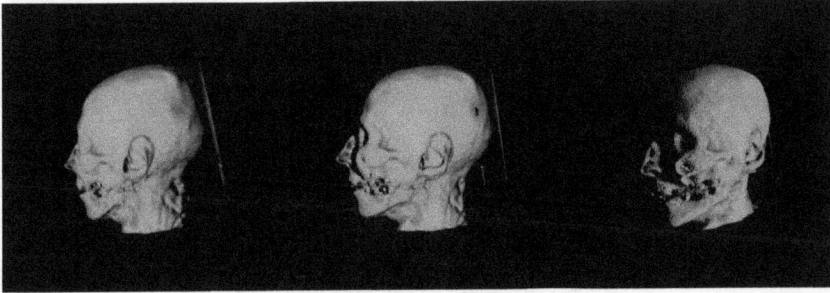

Figure 6.4: Image-based remote rendering of a CT head dataset. Left: the original image before reprojection. Middle: reprojection that was applied due to a slightly altered view point. Holes are visible especially around the nose and the left eye, where no image data from the original view point is available. Right: hole artifacts grow more annoying due to an extreme reprojection.

be implemented as a user-defined parameter that can be adjusted to the specific combination of volume data and transfer function.

The proposed heuristics were designed to handle different scenarios. If the transfer function contains high frequencies, it is likely that a strong isosurface is present that determines the depth values. Other combinations of datasets with transfer functions do not favor strong isosurfaces but extract mostly homogeneous regions. Not all of the various heuristics will be good matches for both extremes. A thorough evaluation of the proposed heuristics follows below in Section 6.5.

6.2.4 Reprojection Artifacts

The proposed reprojection technique is an extreme approximation, which only produces the illusion of actually interacting with the real dataset for slight changes to the camera transform. The method is subject to multiple sources of uncertainty, which will result in visually disturbing artifacts. The most obvious artifacts that arise are *holes*, which for the purposes of this work are defined as image pixels for which no image data is available and which are thus, for lack of a better alternative, set to the background color. The remote rendering technique relies on the fact that for the

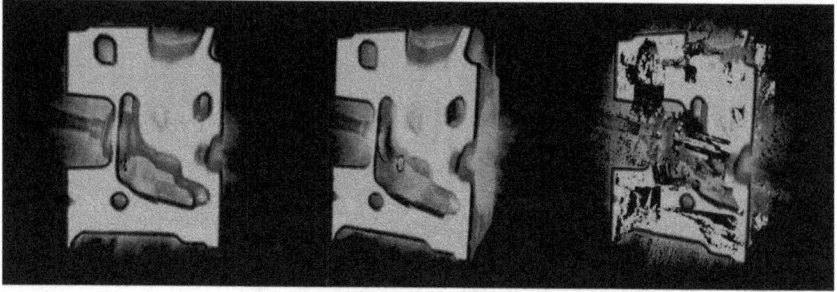

Figure 6.5: This sequence of images shows a case where a depth heuristic produces severe reprojection artifacts. Left: image rendered for the original view point. Middle: exact rendering of the same dataset, but with a slightly altered view point. Right: this image was created by reprojecting the 2.5D dataset representation depicted on the left side to the view point of the image in the middle. The Peak heuristic was used to generate the depth buffer for the 2.5D dataset. The right image showcases jumping artifacts that arise due to the fact that the Peak heuristic does not take cumulative effects along the ray into account.

course of only a few frames and view point changes, e. g. due to slight movements of the head in a Virtual Reality application, these artifacts are negligible. When the difference between current and original view points increase, whole regions of connected holes arise and the illusion of actually interacting with the real dataset instead of with a 2.5D image-based approximation diminishes. Figure 6.4 illustrates how those artifacts grow more severe, the more the current and the original camera transforms diverge.

Artifacts may also arise if the heuristic employed for depth buffer generation on the server is insufficient for the dataset. The generated depth buffer in general is subject to errors originating from the trade-off between execution times and quality. Two-pass heuristics require the dataset to be rendered twice on the server-side but tend to produce results with a higher quality than those obtainable through single-pass heuristics. Apart from that, some of the heuristics introduced in Subsection 6.2.3 favor volume dataset and transfer function combinations with certain characteristics like an easily extractable isosurface or a large amount of transparency that is assigned homogeneously to all data items by the transfer function, regardless of their data

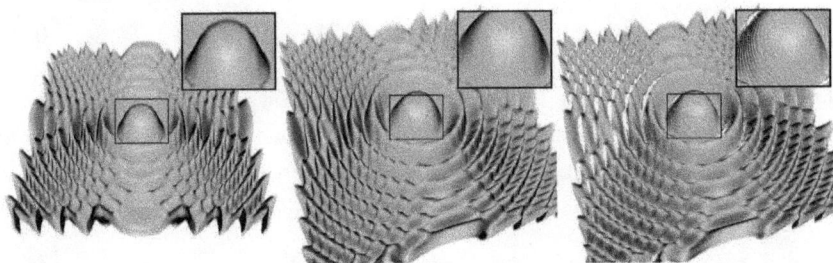

Figure 6.6: The left and middle images show correct renderings of the Marschner Lobb test dataset [ML94]. The right image was rendered using the reprojection technique with depth values generated by using the *Relative Threshold* heuristic. In the right image, artifacts are visible that are due to samples generated for incorrect lighting conditions. Especially the highlights resulting from local illumination calculations for *specular* lighting are implausible. The magnified views show a highlight where this problem is most obvious.

value. Figure 6.5 shows an image exhibiting strong artifacts that arise due to an inappropriate depth heuristic that jumps between isosurfaces at different depths.

Another source of artifacts, that every remote rendering application is potentially subject to, are compression artifacts that occur when the image stream is encoded using a lossy compression algorithm. The IBR-based technique proposed in this thesis is subject to compression artifacts even to a higher degree, because not only the 2D image, but also the depth buffer is potentially compressed using a lossy algorithm. Subsection 6.3.3 outlines compression schemes that specifically apply to depth values.

Artifacts may also arise from reflections that were approximated using a reflectance model simulating mere local illumination. In particular, specular highlights are only valid for the view point before warping, but not for the new view point (cf. Figure 6.6). Reflectance models like the Phong model [Pho75] typically add diffuse and specular contributions to the sample color. The color contribution due to diffuse reflection is then approximated using Lambert's formula

$$C_{diffuse} = (N \cdot L) K_d \qquad (6.4)$$

for positive angles between the unit vector to the light source L and the normal vector at the sample position N, where Kd is a diffuse material property. In contrast to the diffuse contribution, which only depends on the position of the light source and on the sample position, the specular contribution is also view point-dependent:

$$C_{specular} = (V \cdot N)^n K_s, \qquad (6.5)$$

where V is a unit vector to the viewing position and K_s the material property that represents the specular reflection. This general behavior holds true for most other reflectance models that take specular reflection into account [Bli77] [CT82] [War92] [LFTG97]. Using the proposed technique in conjunction with such a reflectance model thus may produce implausible images.

Because of these shortcomings, the image-based rendering technique is only applicable for interactive applications which suffer from latency that only necessitates a few frames to be approximated. If the two view points differ to much, the resulting reprojection will become implausible. Section 6.3 proposes approaches to conceal the various kinds or mitigate the effects of the artifacts described in this section to enhance the credibility of the reprojected images.

6.2.5   Performance Penalties

Although the image-based remote rendering technique was designed to actually *hide* latency, the algorithm itself may impose several sources of overhead. On the server, on the one hand evaluating the various heuristics to deduce the artificial depth buffer results in overhead during rendering. Evidently, especially the two-pass heuristics suffer from this shortcoming. On the other hand, compressing the resulting buffers and sending them to the client over the network connection is a cause of increased overall time consumption.

Conversely, on the client side, the overhead for image retrieval and decompression is effectively hidden behind computation because of the asynchronous nature of the image-based technique. Here, in comparison to mere remote rendering without latency hiding through warping, performance pressure arises from the geometry setup. The number of primitives that must be rendered grows linearly with the targeted screen resolution. Up until now, the assumption was made that dimensionless point primitives that occupy a single pixel on the screen were used to represent the warped points. In general, enhancements to the trivial algorithm are imaginable that soften this restriction, so that primitives may occupy more than a single screen pixel. In that case, care must be taken to avoid tremendous performance pressure due to an increasing amount of fragments that need to be processed. However, with the unified shader architectures implemented by modern GPUs, a workload imbalance due to uneven geometry and fragment distribution is not to be expected.

6.3 Enhancements to the Remote Rendering Technique

This section proposes several enhancements to the image-based remote rendering technique from above. On the one hand, approaches are presented to enhance the quality and credibility of the generated images on the client side, while on the other hand strategies are proposed that help to improve the overall performance of the remote rendering system. The described techniques tackle the issues reported in Section 6.2.4 and in Section 6.2.5.

6.3.1 Server-Side Latency Hiding

While the image-based remote rendering technique on the client is asynchronous by design, the server-side may suffer from performance issues due to additional overhead that is not related to rendering. The influence of these performance penalties, which originate from image compression and sending the compressed data over the network, can be hidden by performing rendering and the aforementioned tasks asynchronously

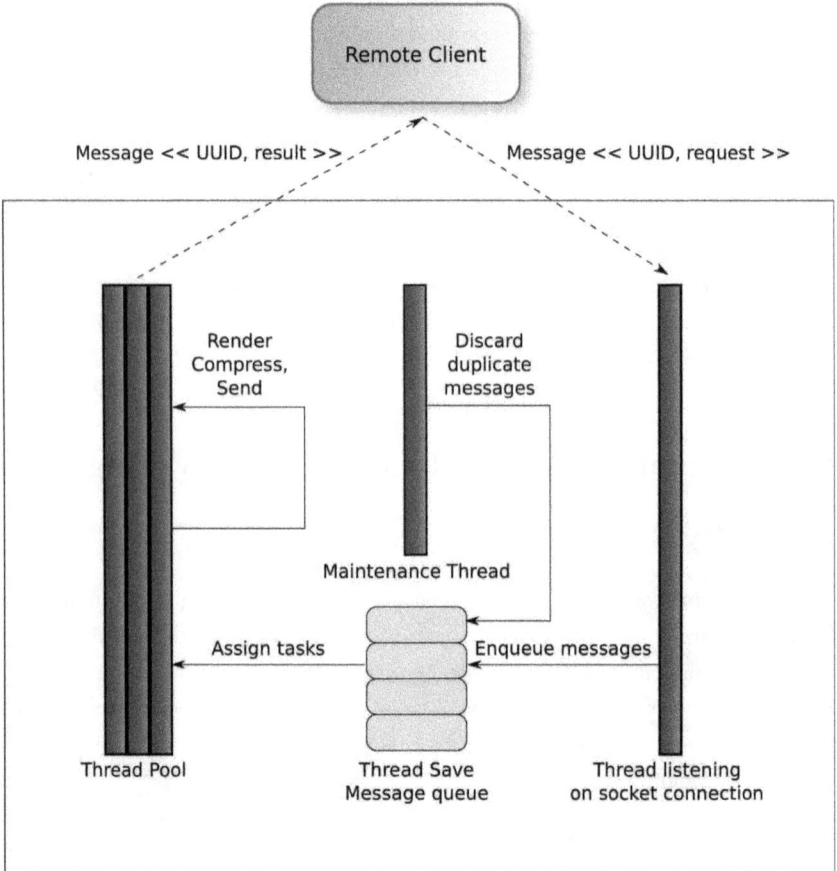

Figure 6.7: Asynchronous event system on the server. The event system was designed to interleave image compression and socket communication from an earlier rendering request with computations from the current request. As a side effect, using a maintenance thread for the message queue, duplicate requests can be discarded.

as well. This demands for an event system that can handle asynchronous requests on the server, because in general one cannot predict how rendering and sending for subsequent requests interleave. Figure 6.7 depicts the workflow of the asynchronous event system that was integrated into the Virvo DVR library. The asynchronous event system is centered around a server class that basically consists of a thread safe queue that collects incoming messages. Each message is associated with a unique identifier and a token that can be translated to an event. Objects of the server class can handle multiple incoming connections which are also distinguished based on unique identifiers. Server instances are implemented using subclasses that implement a virtual handler function that processes the events. An image-based remote server may e. g. handle the render event in a different way than a mere remote rendering server does, since it must provide a depth buffer for the rendered image. The abstract server object uses one thread to maintain the state of the message queue. That thread performs the *select* system call to read messages from the connected sockets. It then enqueues the retrieved messages into the synchronized queue. During the course of that, a simple optimization is possible. If several messages were issued that demand for the same event to be handled, only one message needs to be kept in the queue and the others may be discarded. That way, several render events can e. g. be merged to a single render event. Messages can now be consumed by multiple threads. While one thread may e. g. be concerned with rendering, another thread can send image data to the client asynchronously. That way, all the latency that is associated with remote rendering can be hidden behind rendering, which is usually the most time-consuming task. In the latter case, the time it takes for an image to be displayed by the client after control information like camera matrices and viewport was sent, is effectively bound by the time it takes for rendering.

The proposed optimization scheme - hiding overhead due to compression and communication behind an ensuing rendering task - is crucial for the image-based remote rendering technique to be effective. Additional sources of increased overhead, nevertheless, are the two-pass heuristics incorporated with the hope to generate more reliable depth buffers. Because the two passes are dependent, they cannot be performed asynchronously. Nevertheless, since the color buffer is already created after the first rendering pass, the workflow could be further rectified by sending the color buffer asynchronously immediately after the first rendering pass, and thus only having to send the depth buffer after the second rendering pass. Nevertheless, this type of optimization will be less effective when performed in conjunction with hiding compression and communication behind the ensuing rendering event and is thus noted for future work.

6.3.2   Corrections for Local Illumination

Renderings with a reflection model applied suffer from inconsistencies because the angle between the surface normal and the light vector goes into these calculations and generally differs per view point. A fix for this behavior can be implemented by deferring the lighting calculations to image space. Then, the normals are calculated per sampling position, but rather than performing lighting calculations with them immediately, they are temporarily accumulated, like colors and opacities are. The accumulated normals can then be transferred to the client in an additional buffer. This accumulation process can be implemented in different ways, where each implementation is a heuristic again. Pure averaging of the normals may e. g. be undesirable if a strong isosurface is extracted from the data. Then it would be a more intuitive approach to accumulate the normal by favoring sampling positions near the isosurface over sampling positions that are farther away. Choosing an appropriate normal accumulation heuristic is a similar task to choosing a heuristic for depth buffer extraction. A formal analysis of those heuristics and the general fitness of the deferred lighting calculation approach is, nevertheless, out of the scope of this thesis and remains future work.

After transferring the normal buffer to the client, the shading calculations are performed per vertex. In general, any reflection model can be applied to the 2.5D data. The shaded color can then be blended with the color buffer from the server, which accounts for an evaluation of the volume rendering integral with absorption and emission and source and extinction terms obtained through the application of a post-classification transfer function.

Though this procedure will produce more accurate results because the lighting calculations match the current viewing configuration, the bandwidth pressure that it implies renders this procedure inapplicable if implemented naively. In order to reduce this bandwidth pressure, several optimizations can be applied.

Normals are direction vectors. So, in contrast to storing normals in cartesian coordinates, a representation in polar coordinates reduces the amount of floating-point variables per normal from 3 to 2 and thus the memory demand per normal from 12 bytes to 8 bytes. The memory demand can be further reduced by storing the normals with half-float precision, i. e. with 16 bits per floating-point value instead of 32 bits. Storing normals with a precision as low as 8 bits was shown to be sufficient for surface rendering in the past [Mit07]. Assuming that normals are largely coherent over smooth surfaces, the size of the normal buffer could be drastically reduced by using downscaling, so that the same normal is e. g. assigned to a screen space region of 4×4 neighboring image fragments. By combining these approaches with ordinary compression algorithms, the bandwidth impact of sending an additional normal buffer over the network can be dramatically reduced.

6.3.3   Depth Buffer Compression

Depth buffers demand compression schemes that differ e. g. from the chrominance / luminance-based compression algorithms that are used for RGB images. There exist a number of patents that describe efficient depth compression algorithms. This is mainly due to the fact that depth buffer compression is of interest for the graphic card vendors who have a need to incorporate depth buffer compression into their GPUs. Hasselgren and Akenine-Möller summarized some of the algorithms [HAM06]. Most of the algorithms are based on processing tiles, which is reasonable e. g. in cases where a sort-middle approach (cf. Section 3.4.1) is used. A common scheme of the algorithms is to define some proxy, such as a plane, that interpolates the depth field of the respective tile. The depth buffer can then be stored as offsets to the proxy. Assuming a sufficiently coherent depth buffer, the offsets can be stored with a much lower precision than the original depth values.

For this thesis, anyhow, the implementation of a dedicated compression algorithm remains future work. Nevertheless, sending a raw depth buffer is not an option because this can result in a multiple of the bandwidth consumption compared to sending only compressed RGB images. Because of that, several image compression algorithms were evaluated to compress the depth buffer. PNG, a lossless image compression algorithm and Snappy, a general compression algorithm, both provide reasonable compression ratios and fast encoding and decoding. In order to obtain the performance measurements from Section 6.5.1, the Snappy compression algorithm was used, because this lossless technique proved to deliver good compression ratios at high compression and decompression speeds. An evaluation of various image compression algorithms for depth buffers can also be found in Section 6.5.1.

6.4   Application to Virtual Reality

In Virtual Reality (VR) applications, the position of the user is usually tracked and thus the camera configuration needs to be adjusted continuously. Drops in frame rates due to latency or halts are intolerable because they are one cause of the motion sickness that users of VR applications often suffer from. The image-based rendering technique is a perfect match for VR applications because it can effectively hide latency.

The image-based rendering technique was integrated into the VR renderer COVER, which is part of the COVISE visualization software (cf. Section 3.5.6). COVER executes only the display phase of the Distributed Volume Rendering Pipeline, while the previous stages run in a separate server program that ships with the Virvo library.

An integral part of VR applications are stereo rendering capabilities. Stereo rendering creates the illusion that the projection to the 2D image plane is actually three-dimensional by overlaying one image per eye with an adjusted perspective, and then filtering the respective content using glasses. Two stereo rendering modes are common:

Passive Stereo. Two perspectives are overlaid *"in space"* and later separated using the polarization properties of light. A spatial overlay means that image space is subdivided among the two perspectives so that each rendered image occupies half of the available pixels. The composited image containing the two perspectives is then projected onto a screen or canvas with a polarization filter attached to it. The glasses are equipped with filters that have matching polarization. That way, the respective image is redirected to the appropriate eye by blocking all the light that comes from the image for the other eye.

Active Stereo. This stereo mode is based on a *"time overlay"*. Two perspectives are rendered one after another and are displayed at high refresh rates of 100 Hz and beyond. *Shutter glasses* operate at the same frequency that the display device does and alternatingly shut out all light that belongs to the left eye and to the right eye. The stereo mode is said to be active because the glasses need a power supply. Synchronization between the glasses and the display device is accomplished by using a synchronizer which is hooked up to the graphics card of the rendering computer. The graphics card typically has to support active stereo by providing compatibility with the synchronizer, and by providing the ability to render to disjoint memory buffers for the left and the right eye.

COVER supports both stereo modes. The IBR technique was implemented in an active stereo scenario using a Full HD powerwall and optical tracking of the user's head. The user can also use a tracked pointing device that is equipped with mouse buttons. The active stereo scenario is the easier one to implement, because it does not require asynchronous execution. Because of the time overlay paradigm, frames are rendered consecutively. With an asynchronous execution mode, the IBR technique is harder to implement because there would be two processes that are each attached to a server process. With these two server processes, that each operate independently, in general the two 2.5D approximate images will not match and the illusion of 3D viewing would thus be disturbed. With active stereo and consecutive execution, this problem is largely mitigated. This is because the instances in time that the two eyes are served with new images can be easily synchronized by means of the asynchronous message system. A timestamp can be attached to the messages, and rendering requests are only processed if there is another rendering request with the same timestamp. With VR scenarios where two display clients are served by two independent server processes, this synchronization must be implemented using interprocess communication.

6.5   Results

The evaluation of the image-based remote rendering technique for DVR was conducted based on several criteria. A performance analysis outlines *timing and bandwidth* tests. A *perceptual* evaluation gives insight in how the various heuristics to extract a depth buffer from volumes perform with different combinations of volume datasets and transfer functions. The perceptual analysis contrasts the amount of visual artifacts in terms of holes, which will affect the user experience through flickering, with the faithfulness of the reconstruction, which is important in the context of scientific visualization.

6.5.1   Performance Analysis

This section considers the image-based remote rendering technique from a performance view point. The algorithm was evaluated in terms of the overhead that is imposed by sending a depth buffer in contrast to sending only RGB images, and in terms of the performance penalties imposed by rendering points instead of mere image pixels. The time consumed by the remote rendering algorithm is divided into three periods which can in parts be interleaved. On the *server-side*, on top of the time it takes to generate an image using DVR, overhead occurs due to depth buffer generation, potentially due to a second rendering pass, and also due to compressing the image buffer and the depth buffer. After compression, the image needs to be sent over the *network*. On the *client-side*, the buffers are received, and additional overhead compared to mere image rendering occurs due to the high geometry load imposed by the image-based rendering technique itself. These three phases - *server-side, network transfer* and *client-side* - were analyzed as follows.

Different compression algorithms were considered. The overhead on the server-side was considered by measuring the time it takes to compress the buffers based on

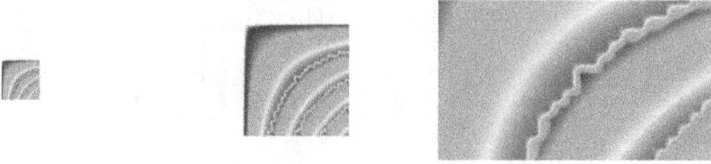

Figure 6.8: Test volume that was used to evaluate the depth buffer compression using various image compression algorithms. In the following, the three view points will be referred to as Far (left), Default (center), and Near (right).

the type of compression algorithm used. On the client, the time was measured that it takes to decompress the buffers, and the time it takes to render the point cloud associated with the buffers. The time it takes to transfer the image data and depth buffer over the network is harder to separate. Network transfers are usually implemented as *streams* by the operating system and the networking APIs. This implies that library calls to send data are implemented as non-blocking functions which return immediately, while asynchronously streaming the data to be sent to the network connection. A reliable measurement of the actual time it takes to send data over the network is thus hard to achieve, specifically if the data transfer only takes split seconds. Furthermore, the time overhead is largely due to the available bandwidth that the network connection supplies, which is subject to several influencing factors which are outside the scope of the algorithm. Because of that, to judge the overhead imposed on the network connection, the compression ratio of the different compression techniques was measured as an *absolute* indicator of the overhead imposed by the network transfer. In order to measure the overall performance of the remote rendering algorithm and its latency, the rate at which new depth images are received from the server was measured (for those timing results, see Table 6.6 and the detailed description of the timing procedure below).

For the performance measurements, three different types of compression were applied to the depth images: PNG image compression, Snappy compression and JPEG image compression. All tests were performed on an Intel® Core™ i7 920 CPU running Ubuntu Linux 12.04 with Linux kernel 3.2.0-39. All software packages were built using the GNU compiler toolchain version 4.6.3. Further, the PNG library, version

View Point	Depth	Depth (kB)	Image	Image (kB)
Far	200.00	10	71.43	117
Default	62.50	33	14.29	566
Near	40.00	50	6.67	1217

Table 6.1: Compression ratios for the three view points from Figure 6.8, obtained using the PNG algorithm. Compression ratios are presented along with the absolute size of the compressed buffer.

View Point	Depth	Depth (kB)	Image	Image (kB)
Far	19.23	105	13.33	610
Default	14.93	135	4.35	1865
Near	12.99	156	2.02	4010

Table 6.2: Compression ratios obtained using the Snappy algorithm.

1.2.46 [Roe14], and the Snappy library, version 1.0.4-1 [Goo14], were used. For JPEG compression, libjpeg-turbo, version 1.1.90 [Com14a], was used. In contrast to the PNG and Snappy implementations, the JPEG implementation is optimized for several SIMD instruction sets, including the SSE instruction set provided by the Intel CPU used for the performance measurements. The measurements were performed for an artificial test dataset viewed from different camera positions (cf. Figure 6.8). These positions were chosen to include a varying amount of actual depth pixels and of holes. The *"compression level"* is a parameter to the PNG algorithm which trades off compression ratio for compression and decompression speed. For this performance analysis, the compression level, which ranges from 0 to 9, was set to 5. The lossy JPEG compression algorithm was configured to use a quality of 75 %.

View Point	Depth	Depth (kB)	Image	Image (kB)
Far	62.50	32	125.00	64
Default	31.25	64	62.50	128
Near	62.50	32	62.50	128

Table 6.3: Compression ratios obtained using the JPEG algorithm.

View Point	PNG		Snappy		JPEG	
	Depth	Image	Depth	Image	Depth	Image
Far	49.7	215.2	1.1	7.8	8.9	11.7
Default	49.0	312.5	1.4	11.4	9.6	12.4
Near	48.9	559.6	1.7	26.2	9.3	12.7

Table 6.4: Average time in milliseconds for compressing the three Full HD images from Figure 6.8 using PNG, Snappy, and JPEG.

View Point	PNG		Snappy		JPEG	
	Depth	Image	Depth	Image	Depth	Image
Far	7.7	37.5	1.7	6.2	4.1	7.8
Default	9.5	62.9	1.4	6.3	4.4	9.5
Near	10.0	62.8	1.8	13.9	4.3	11.1

Table 6.5: Average time in milliseconds for decompressing the three Full HD images from Figure 6.8 using PNG, Snappy, and JPEG.

Tables 6.1, 6.2, and 6.3 summarize the compression ratios (size of uncompressed data over size of compressed data) of the algorithms for the three camera positions. The measurements were performed for a viewport size of 1920×1080 pixels (Full HD). An uncompressed depth image of that size amounts to $8,100$ kB for the 32 bit image buffer and $2,025$ kB for the 8 bit depth buffer. Table 6.4 lists the time that compression took for the three view points, and Table 6.5 summarizes the amount of time necessary for decompression. Of highest interest are the performance measurements for the depth buffer, while the results for the image buffers are included for completeness. All *timing* results were averaged over a representative amount of frames. The timing procedure itself was implemented using the *high_resolution_clock* class from the C++ Library *Boost::Chrono* for high-precision timing results.

The JPEG algorithm is the only lossy compression technique that was used for the comparison. JPEG has two significant shortcomings in the context of image-based remote volume rendering. On the one hand, JPEG does not support images with an alpha channel, so that opacity needs to be transferred along with the depth images in a separate buffer. This is relevant if the rendered volume shall be composited on

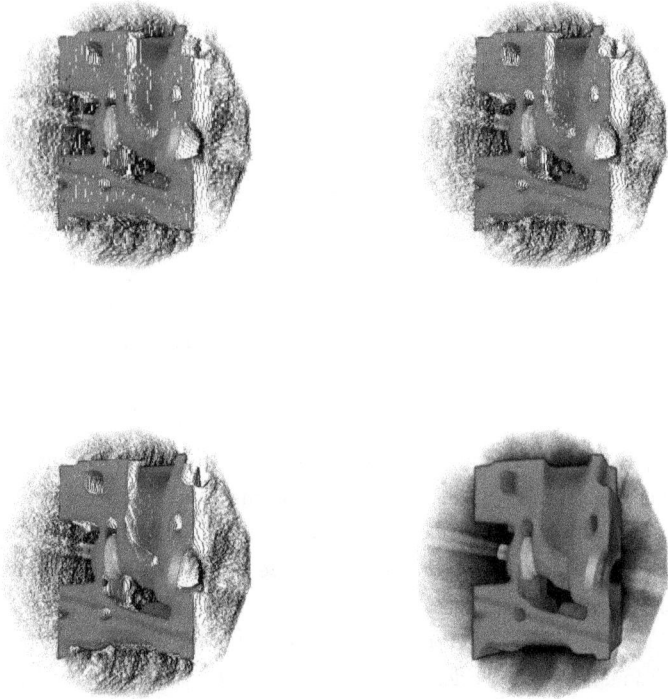

Figure 6.9: Comparing JPEG compression for the depth buffer to lossless compression. All color buffers were compressed using the lossless Snappy algorithm. Depth buffers were compressed, from left to right, top to bottom: JPEG, 25% quality, JPEG, 75% quality, Snappy (lossless), DVR rendering w/o 2.5D data for comparison.

Dataset	Frames Rendered / sec.	Frames Received / sec.
Artificial	29.1	29.1
CT-Head	16.6	16.6
Visible Human	23.3	23.3

Table 6.6: Frame rates at which images for the three test datasets were generated on the server, and frame rates at which they were received on the client. The update rates are virtually indistinguishable, which shows that server-side latency hiding is an effective means to conceal remote rendering overhead for compressing images on the server and sending them over the network.

top of some other geometry such as an isosurface. For the course of the performance tests, this modality was neglected, but needs to be considered if DVR is performed as part of a visualization which combines different rendering techniques. On the other hand, artifacts that JPEG compression introduces are considered to be acceptable for RGB images, while this in general is not true for depth buffers. Figure 6.9 shows compressed depth buffers with different JPEG qualities, compared to lossless depth buffer compression and a DVR image for completeness. The typical block artifacts known from JPEG compression for RGB images are especially disturbing with the compressed depth buffer.

Although the compression ratios obtained with the PNG algorithm were superior to those obtained using Snappy or JPEG, the compression speed was inapplicable for interactive scenarios, even if the overhead is hidden e. g. behind rendering on the server. PNG compression is thus only an option if interactive frame rates are of lower importance than bandwidth issues, e. g. if rendering is performed using a wide area network (WAN). Equally general, one may say that the lossless Snappy algorithm is competitive, even if compared to the lossy JPEG algorithm, and renders it a potent candidate for use in interactive environments. Most specifically, the Snappy algorithm proved to be superior at compressing and decompressing the depth buffer, even if compared to dedicated image compression algorithms like JPEG. Note that these findings not necessarily hold true for image compression, where the JPEG algorithm, when disregarding its impact on image quality, is superior to Snappy compression in several cases.

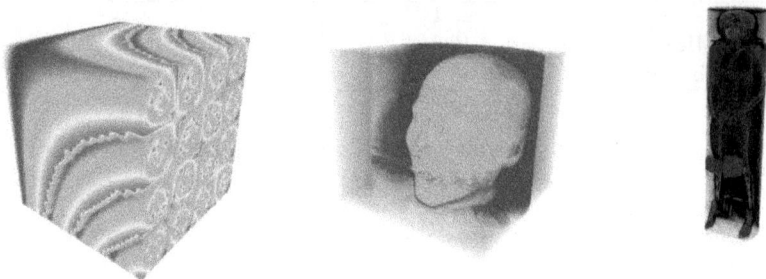

Figure 6.10: Three datasets used to evaluate the IBR technique. From left to right: Artificial dataset (32 x 32 x 32 voxels), CT-Head dataset (256 x 256 x 225 voxels), Visible Human dataset (512 x 512 x 1877 voxels).

Because of its good results for image compression and its general superiority for depth buffer compression, the subsequent performance tests were based on compression of both the image data and the depth buffer using the Snappy algorithm. The IBR technique was evaluated using several timing procedures. To conduct the tests, a server computer and a desktop client were used. Both computers had Ubuntu Linux 12.04 with Linux kernel 3.2.0-39 installed. The server computer was equipped with two physical CPUs of type Intel® Xeon™ E5-2690, which can each run eight concurrent threads through multi-core and hyper-threading technologies. The client was equipped with an an Intel® Core™ i7 920 CPU. The server computer was equipped with four NVIDIA® GeForce GTX Titan™ GPUs. However, for the ensuing tests, only one of the GPUs was actually used. The two computers communicated over an ethernet connection with a maximum bandwidth of 1 Gbit/s. Image-based remote rendering was performed. For the performance tests, the two-pass heuristic *Relative Threshold* (cf. Section 6.2.3) was used to generate the depth buffer. The three configurations depicted in Figure 6.10 were used to conduct the tests. The timing procedure was the same as the one outlined in Section 5.4: frame rates were averaged over a sequence of 270 rendered frames. The sequence rotated the volume about the principal axes in world coordinates, with a slight, random deviance about the two remaining axes. Viewports of size 1920×1080 pixels (Full

Dataset	Color and Depth Texture Update Time (ms)
Artificial	4.6
CT-Head	4.2
Visible Human	4.2

Table 6.7: The time it takes to update the two textures that supply colors and depth to the IBR shader for Full HD viewports. As expected, these times are independent of the dataset size.

HD) were considered.

Table 6.6 outlines the actual frame rates that it took to render on the server and compares it to the rate at which the frames were received at the client. The results show that the rendering speed is proportional to the rate at which new frames are received on the client. For typical dataset sizes like the ones used for the performance tests, due to hiding latency behind rendering on the server side and the fast decompression that the Snappy algorithm provides, there is thus no significant extra overhead that arises due to using the remote rendering implementation.

After receiving the 2.5D dataset, the next step comprises updating of the color texture and the depth texture, and actually rendering the point cloud. The following timing results were obtained by applying the same test procedure like the one described above. Several OpenGL function calls, like the ones to update texture buffers, or those to render vertex buffer objects, are non-blocking and execution immediately returns after the call was issued. To obtain correct timing results, OpenGL *synchronization fences* were used, which basically are barriers which are waited upon until all previous GPU events finished execution. As can be seen from Table 6.7, updating the color and depth textures on an NVIDIA® GeForce™ GPU takes approximately 4 ms, independent of the size of the dataset rendered.

Table 6.8 shows the average time it takes to render the point buffers for the three test datasets. Once again, rendering times are not bound by the size of the dataset. In comparison to the rate at which frames are rendered, new images are received rather infrequently. As a coarse approximation based on the timing results, three frames are displayed using warping, while one frame is received and the color and

Dataset	Rendering Times for the Point Buffer (ms)
Artificial	9.6
CT-Head	11.3
Visible Human	11.1

Table 6.8: Time it takes to render Full HD frames using the IBR technique. Once again, the execution times were not bound by the dataset size, which is crucial for the latency hiding technique to be effective.

depth texture are updated accordingly. Because of that, execution is bound by the rendering time of the point buffers. That way, latency can effectively be hidden on the client side.

6.5.2   Error Estimates for the Depth Heuristics

A perceptual analysis of the IBR remote rendering technique was conducted for the conference publication by Zellmann et al., who compared the heuristics for extracting depth buffers from volume datasets in order to judge their fitness for different combinations of volume datasets and transfer functions.

Because the 2.5D technique can only reconstruct parts of the artificial world that the depth images were generated for, an error analysis must take two variables into account. On the one hand, it is of interest for the error analysis to judge how *faithfully* an unbiased rendering can be reconstructed from the 2.5D data. On the other hand, a qualitative analysis will typically take into account to which degree the approximate image is biased by visual *artifacts* due to holes. Hole artifacts, though displeasing, will not conceal actual facts. They just occur due to no sufficient data being available to render a specific region of the image. They thus cannot solely serve as the basis for a qualitative judgment of the depth heuristic used to generate the image. The faithfulness of the reconstruction on the other hand is directly influenced by the reliability of the depth heuristic to place a fragment of the 2.5D dataset at an appropriate z-position. The color contribution along a ray is typically influenced by few *features* encountered along the ray. If the z-position happens to be completely misplaced in regard to that feature, one may deem the reconstruction to be unfaithful.

On the other hand, since the image-based rendering technique is usually used for latency hiding, visually disturbing artifacts may very well be judged as important an issue as unfaithful results, because the incorrect frame will typically only be viewed for the fraction of a second. In that case, hole artifacts will manifest themselves as *flickering*. This aliasing artifact is due to the fact that features that are not visible in one image suddenly become visible in the next.

For their evaluation of the various heuristics in terms of their faithfulness, the authors used the *Peak Signal-To-Noise-Ratio* error metric (converted to dB) of the resulting images

$$PSNR_i = 10 \cdot log10 \left(\frac{MAX_T^2}{MSE_i} \right), \tag{6.6}$$

where MSI_i is the *mean squared error* of the image and MAX_T is the maximum noise. The noise, that is used to calculate the mean squared error, was determined by subtraction of pixel intensities. For that, original images were rendered using the IBR technique. The depth images obtained by this procedure were warped using tiny changes in the viewing angle. The resulting, warped images were then compared to reference images that were obtained by ordinary renderings for the same viewing configuration.

PSNR in general is known to fail as a reliable error metric in certain situations, specifically if the contents compared differ to much [HTG08]. PSNR is typically used when e. g. a compression codec is compared to a raw image. On the other hand, because PSNR is a noise metric based on image pixel comparison, comparing content *known* to be identical will also obscure the results. For example, if two renderings of a dataset, which were compressed using two different codecs, are compared, and the rendered objects are viewed from afar, most of the image pixels will be assigned the background color. Comparing the two images will probably give a high PSNR of nearly 30 dB, but this result will not be meaningful because the known similarities obscure the differences one is typically interested in.

So, in order to obtain meaningful results, for the conference proceeding and for the results that were collected for this thesis, not the PSNR for whole images was

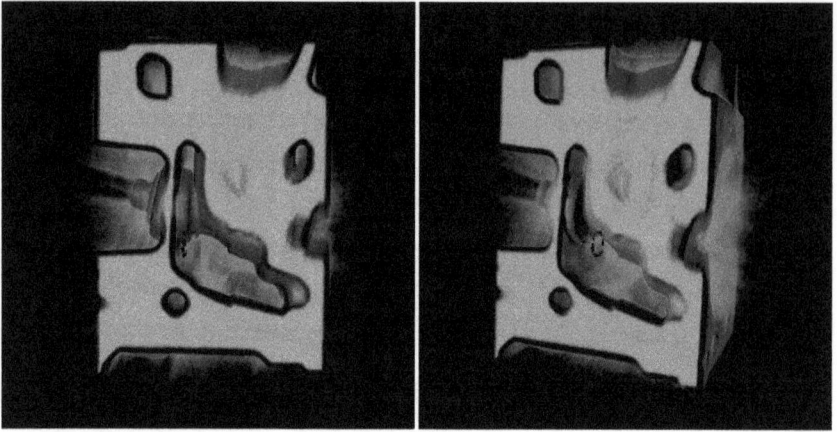

Figure 6.11: Original position and expected outcome for the test scenario with a transfer function that extracts an isosurface from the test dataset. This figure was originally published in [ZAL12] and is reprinted with friendly permission of ASME.

compared, but only for those image pixels that have an actual depth value associated with it. Per definition, this is true for those pixels that are not holes, and thus also for those pixels that were not assigned the background color because the ray used for integration missed the bounding box of the volume. That way, not only could a reliable judgment be achieved that is based on PSNR. Furthermore, the analysis could be separated in terms of the two variables that influence the quality of the reconstruction: visually displeasing artifacts and actual reconstruction errors due to miscalculation. That way, the *rectified* PSNR could be used to judge the faithfulness of the reconstruction, and the relative amount of holes could be used to judge its *visual quality*.

Two configurations were used to evaluate the various depth heuristics, which are shown in Figure 6.11 and 6.12. The dataset used to perform the evaluation is the General Electric engine dataset that is freely available for scientific studies on the internet [Uni06]. Two types of different transfer functions were designed to reconstruct information of interest from the volume dataset. Figure 6.11 shows a transfer function that extracts a strong isosurface from the data. Figure 6.12 shows

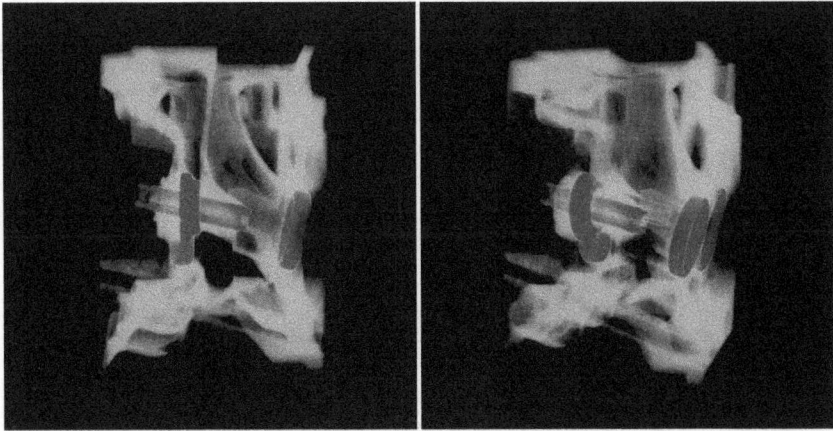

Figure 6.12: Original position and expected outcome for the test scenario with a transfer function that favors mostly transparent features. This figure was originally published in [ZAL12] and is reprinted with friendly permission of ASME.

a setup with a transfer function that maps low opacity values to data items, so that the choice of a suitable z-position for the 2.5D fragment certainly will be more ambiguous than with the isosurface setup.

Both test setups were subjected to the test scenario in the same way. First the volume was rotated and translated to its initial position which is depicted on the left sides of both Figure 6.11 and 6.12. A 2.5D image was rendered for the initial position, which was then warped by 20° about the y axis of the object coordinate system. On the right side of both figures, the unbiased outcome is depicted after not warping the intermediate representation, but rotating the actual dataset. This test procedure was carried out for the depth heuristics proposed in Section 6.2.3, which were each applied to both test scenarios. The heuristics *Threshold* and *Relative Threshold* accumulate opacity up to a certain amount. In the case of the *Threshold* heuristic, for the evaluation opacity was accumulated up to 80 %, and in the case of the *Relative Threshold* heuristic, during the second rendering pass, opacity was accumulated up to 80 % of the opacity that was evaluated along the ray during the first rendering pass.

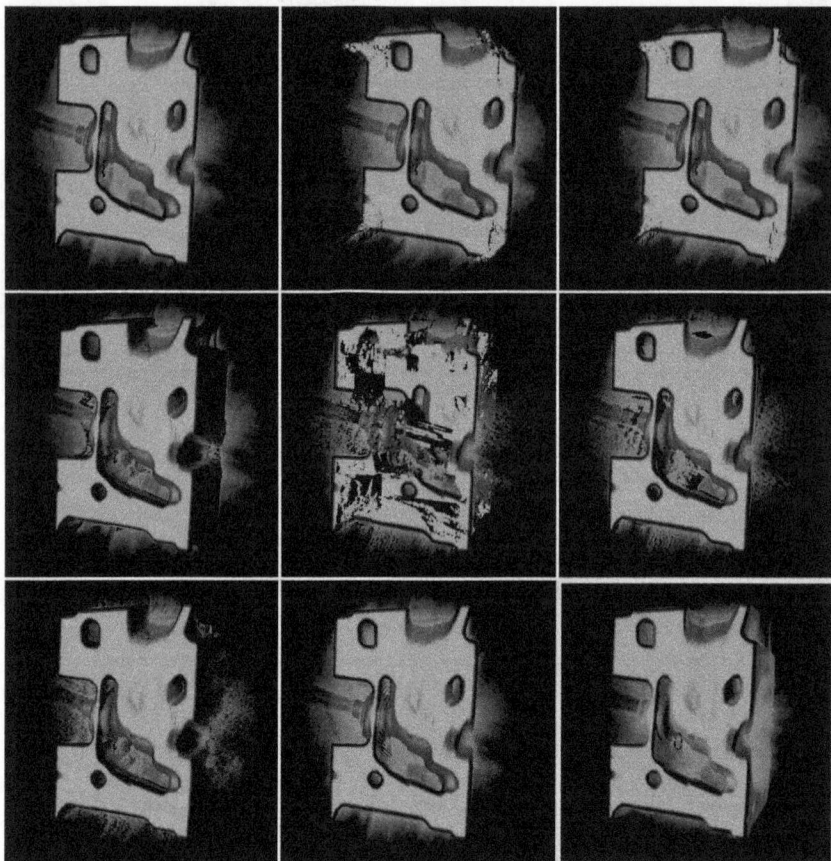

Figure 6.13: Results for the isosurface scenario. First and second row: single-pass heuristics. Third row: two-pass heuristics. From left to right - first row: Entry, Exit and Midpoint heuristics. Second row: Threshold, Peak and Gradient heuristics. Third row: Relative Threshold and Entry / Exit Mean heuristics. The highlighted image in the lower right corner depicts the unbiased outcome after a rotation instead of a warp transformation. This figure was originally published in [ZAL12] and is reprinted with friendly permission of ASME.

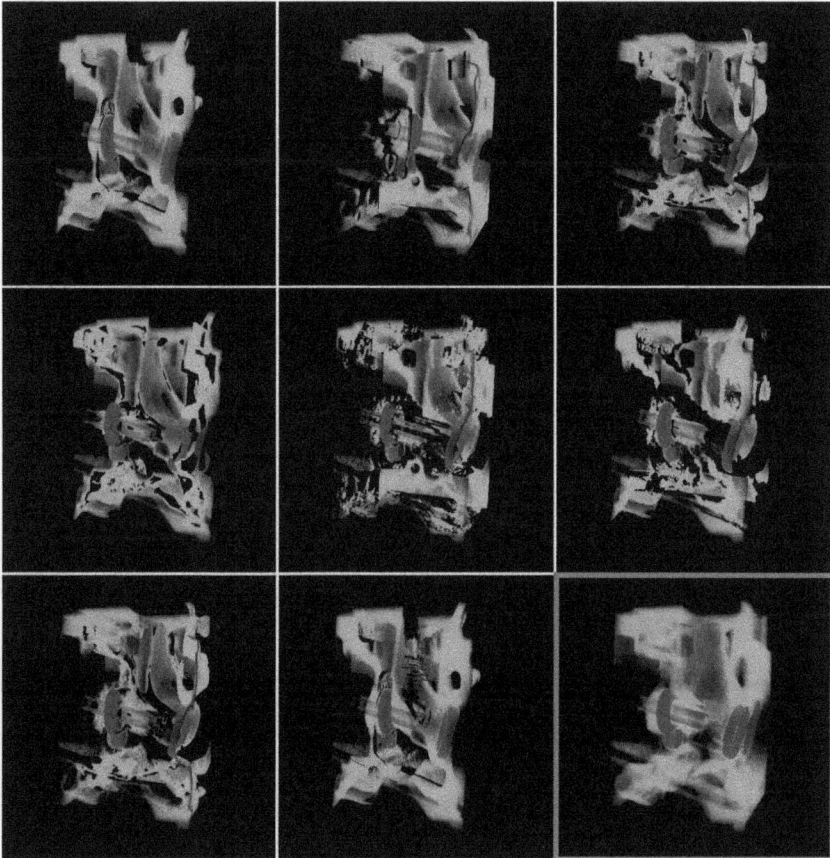

Figure 6.14: Results for the scenario with a transfer function assigning low opacity to the data items. See the caption for Figure 6.13 for the assignment of result images to depth heuristics. The highlighted image was again obtained by rotating the original dataset instead of warping the 2.5D approximate rendering. This figure was originally published in [ZAL12] and is reprinted with friendly permission of ASME.

Heuristic	PSNR (dB)	Holes (%)
Entry	19.52	17
Exit	11.32	20
Midpoint	11.29	13
Threshold	21.2	19
Peak	16.11	30
Gradient	20.55	24
Relative Threshold	21.92	26
Entry / Exit Mean	19.54	18

Table 6.9: Peak Signal-To-Noise Ratios and holes in percent for various depth heuristics applied to the engine dataset with the isosurface extracting transfer function from Figure 6.11. Those results were originally published in [ZAL12] and are reprinted with friendly permission of ASME.

Table 6.9 and 6.10 summarize the results from the conference publication for the two test scenarios. Figures 6.13 and 6.14 show the outcome of the evaluation for both datasets.

For the setup that extracted an isosurface from the dataset, a PSNR greater than 20 *dB* suggests that the most faithful results were obtained using the heuristics *Gradient, Threshold,* and *Relative Threshold.* For the other setup, the heuristics *Threshold* and *Relative Threshold* produced acceptable results. The *Peak* heuristic was specifically insufficient to reconstruct an isosurface because it produced jumping artifacts. In the specific case, these stem from the fact that both the front-side as well as the back-side of the engine have similar material properties and thus compete for the assignment of the peak position. Slight variations would favor the front-side along one ray, and the back-side along the neighboring ray, in an unpredictable manner. The heuristics *Entry, Exit, Midpoint,* and *Entry / Exit Mean* proved unreliable because they tend to map all depth values to a single plane, even if the contour described by an isosurface that was extracted was highly faceted.

Most notably, though producing the most reliable results, the two-pass heuristics did not prove to be absolutely superior to the single-pass heuristics. The *Gradient* heuristic did for certain configurations like the one where a strong isosurface was extractable from the dataset provide acceptable results, but the *Threshold* heuristic

Heuristic	PSNR (dB)	Holes (%)
Entry	15.83	20
Exit	17.26	18
Midpoint	15.94	14
Threshold	18.21	15
Peak	17.96	21
Gradient	16.88	22
Relative Threshold	19.02	28
Entry / Exit Mean	15.48	29

Table 6.10: Peak Signal-To-Noise Ratios and holes in percent for the setup from Figure 6.12. Those results were originally published in [ZAL12] and are reprinted with friendly permission of ASME.

in particular proved to produce acceptable results for general scenarios, even with a lot of transparent data items present.

6.6 Conclusions

The image-based remote rendering technique proposed in this chapter is capable of effectively hiding latency. Because of that, it can be used in interactive scenarios or in virtual environments. With its low demand for compute power, it can be used to perform remote rendering on thin clients such as notebook PCs, or on desktop clients with commodity graphics hardware. On the downside, this flexibility comes at the cost of higher bandwidth consumption due to the depth buffer that must be sent along with the remote rendered image. This penalty can nevertheless be mitigated to a large degree by using compression. The lossless Snappy algorithm proved specifically well suited. The compression ratios that were obtained for compressing the depth buffer using Snappy are superior even to the lossy JPEG format, and the implementation used for this thesis can compress and decompress image buffers and depth buffers at interactive rates.

The image-based rendering technique, though meant to hide latency, actually introduces additional overhead that highly impacts the overall performance of the rendering system if implemented naively. Therefore, in order for the remote rendering technique to become effective, an implementation is mandatory that hides the extra latency behind calculations such as rendering. The proposed implementation accomplishes this by means of an asynchronous event system on the server side.

The effectiveness of the image-based remote rendering technique in conjunction with the asynchronous event system was proved by performing several performance measurements. These showed that the rate at which new images are generated on the server, and the rate at which these new images are received at the client, are mostly identical. Furthermore, rendering Full HD point clouds took only a third of the rate at which Full HD frames were received from the server, so that the technique can be effectively used to hide latency. In general, when rendering at 20 to 30 frames per second, images were received at the same rate. In the meantime, Full HD frames could be rendered by warping the 2.5D intermediate dataset at 90 to 100 frames per second, which is in general sufficient for most interactive applications.

Several enhancements to the image-based rendering algorithm help to conceal visual artifacts. Actual rendering errors nevertheless may have an even higher impact, especially if remote rendering is used to explore a scientific or even medical dataset. Rendering errors are mainly introduced by choosing an inappropriate heuristic to estimate the depth buffer. Several heuristics were evaluated. The evaluation was based on a noise estimator that was adjusted to exclude image regions without a depth contribution. Two-pass heuristics in general proved to be slightly superior to single-pass heuristics. Nevertheless, single-pass heuristics that accumulate opacity or that consider the gradient of the voxel field generally proved to result in an acceptable depth buffer extraction.

Chapter 7

Summary, Conclusions and Future Work

This chapter briefly summarizes and concludes this thesis and gives an outlook on how the methodology that was proposed and evaluated could be developed further. This final chapter is structured as follows. Section 7.1 summarizes the main contributions of this work and outlines their relevance. Section 7.2 summarizes the main conclusions and Section 7.3 gives an outlook on possible future work.

7.1 Contributions and Relevance of this Work

Direct rendering of volumetric phenomena without a prior extraction of a surface representation is highly relevant to several research communities. Meteorologists for example rely on the ability to interactively explore volumetric datasets of weather phenomena [HAF+96]. Two developments could be observed more recently in the context of scientific visualization. On the one hand, the increasing adoption of in situ visualization implies that visualization algorithms are executed on hardware that is no good match for graphic processing. On the other hand, because predictions suggest that the continuous shrinking of transistor sizes will come to a halt in the near future, Moore's law will no longer hold. Even today, the performance increase that was achieved by packing more transistors on a die is no longer realizable and is thus replaced through higher parallelism by the hardware vendors. Those developments are not limited to esoteric hardware such as it is found in HPC systems, but they can already be witnessed in the context of multi-core processors, where the number of cores per processor continuously increased in recent years. Those developments motivate the relevance of the two main contributions of this thesis, i. e. designing and implementing visualization algorithms for highly parallel hardware platforms, and improving remote rendering algorithms which enable visualization algorithms at the same physical location where the simulation is executed.

This work devised a software architecture for distributed volume rendering. The pipeline approach that was proposed is based on the design considerations of Peterka et al. [PRY⁺08], but extends their approach to explicitly support remote rendering scenarios. The display phase of the Distributed Volume Rendering Pipeline is used to divide rendering and display of the scientific dataset and can e. g. be used to implement interactivity techniques.

The two phases of the Distributed Volume Rendering Pipeline that typically impose the highest computational workload are the parallel rendering phase and the display phase. In scenarios which shift the execution of visualization algorithms from client workstations to server computers, the visualization algorithms need to be specifically adapted in order to render with a high quality and at high frame rates. This thesis identified *many-core* systems as the most heterogeneous HPC architecture, which exposes parallelization in different ways. Processing *units* (e. g. CPUs, GPGPUs, or other types of accelerators) were identified to constitute the basic building blocks of many-core systems, and which can be contained by the latter in different combinations. A workload distribution was proposed that assigned rendering tasks to the processing units. Those rendering tasks were executed using sort-first parallel rendering. This design scales to architectures containing many processing units by combining them using sort-last parallel rendering. That way, data parallelism among the processing units can be achieved. Prototypical implementations focused on sort-first rendering, which were targeted towards several hardware platforms.

The display phase, which follows after image compositing, can be implemented to support a variety of different modalities. The scenario targeted in this thesis considered remote rendering with latency from several sources. With the remote rendering approach proposed in this work, it is possible to obtained a fixed frame rate that is independent of the network interconnect between client and server, and of dataset sizes that prohibit interactive rendering. This was achieved by using a reduced dataset for rendering on the client while waiting for new image data. This reduced dataset was built from a 2.5D representation of the most recently obtained image. Several optimizations were proposed, which help to improve the overall quality of the rendered output and the responsiveness of the implementation. Deducing a depth buffer from volume data is only possible using heuristics. Several heuristics were evaluated regarding their fitness for different alpha transfer functions.

7.2 Conclusions

The evaluation of the ray casting algorithm implemented for Intel®-compatible CPUs, for the Intel® Xeon Phi™ coprocessor, and for NVIDIA® GPGPUs revealed the following. In general, the best match for DVR using ray casting is the GPGPU, because of its high memory bandwidth and its hardware support for trilinear texture lookups. However, using SoA-based ray packet traversal, optimized implementations of the ray casting algorithm are at least competitive. For typical dataset sizes, the GPGPU outperforms x86-compatible platforms by factors of 1.5 to 2. The dedicated *gather* instruction that is available on the Intel® Xeon Phi™ can help to dramatically improve the execution of the algorithm. This is promising because future CPU architectures will also support this instruction.

The image-based remote rendering algorithm was evaluated in terms of its performance and in terms of quality. Good performance is crucial for this type of algorithm to actually be *effective*. A method that promises to *hide* latency should only introduce a minimum of extra overhead. This was ensured by means of data compression on the one hand, and server-side latency hiding on the other hand. It was shown that good compression rates for depth buffers can actually be obtained by using image compression algorithms. Server-side latency hiding, which can be viewed as a *double buffering* technique, proved to hide the extra overhead introduced by remote rendering behind calculations that would also have occurred with direct rendering. Various single-pass heuristics were able to produce faithful depth buffers that proved sufficient to give the impression of interacting with actual 3D data over the course of a few frames.

7.3   Outlook

During the work for this thesis, several interesting topics arose that were not investigated in depth. The following list is only an incomplete synopsis of those topics.

The literature on DVR algorithms argues that swizzling can be used for effective cache utilization. Because of that, the SSE code path was adapted to access swizzled volume data. For that, the volume was considered to consist of bricks the size 4^3. In a preprocessing step, the volume was traversed *"brickwise"*, and the data items encountered were flattened to form a contiguous array in main memory. The ray traversal algorithm was then augmented using an index function that matches this altered memory layout. In theory, a bricked memory layout should result in a better cache utilization when combined with the depth-first traversal favored by the ray casting algorithm. The author informally tested the implementation on several contemporary Intel® CPUs, but found it to provide no performance increase over the scanline memory layout that can be implemented more intuitively. However, the evaluation was informal and comprised only contemporary CPUs. It would be interesting to analyze the influence of swizzling on rendering performance on hardware that e. g. does not provide out-of-order instruction execution, like older Intel® Pentium™ CPUs or the Intel® Xeon Phi™.

Knoll et al. [KTW+11] proposed a CPU implementation that, in addition to the early-ray termination optimization, also makes use of the empty-space leaping optimization. To accommodate this optimization, the authors had to favor AoS ray traversal over SoA packet traversal in order to traverse the BVH they used to organize the volume. This approach necessitates the use of a stack to dissolve the recursion necessary to traverse the BVH, with a stack counter maintained per thread. A formal comparison of the two approaches - accepting the additional overhead necessary for BVH traversal or abandoning the use of the empty-space leaping optimization - would be of high interest.

The image-based rendering technique suffers from visual artifacts which arise because the reduced 2.5D dataset does in general not cover the whole screen space for a new camera configuration. The influence of those artifacts could probably be mitigated by using a splatting technique that distributes the color contribution of a pixel over a larger region in screen space. Implementing such a technique would arouse new problems, like artifacts at the boundaries between splats, which would need to be accounted for.

With the proposed configuration, 2.5D image pixel compositing is deferred until the execution of the display phase. However, this thesis only considered that the color and depth buffers were only composited on top of a uniformly colored background. It would be interesting to evaluate the algorithm's usefulness in a sort-last rendering scenario. With an implementation targeted towards sort-last rendering, the 2.5D representation would already have to be accounted for during compositing, i. e. during the execution of the parallel rendering phase of the Distributed Volume Rendering Pipeline.

Obtaining a normal for *faithful* local illumination on the client when using the image-based remote rendering technique can only be done heuristically. While this thesis only suggests some possible implementations for normal accumulation, a formal evaluation like the one conducted for the depth buffer generation heuristics would be an interesting topic to be investigated in the future.

Bibliography

[ABW⁺13]   Sean Ahern, Eric Brugger, Brad Whitlock, Jeremy S. Meredith, Kathleen Biagas, Mark C. Miller, and Hank Childs. Visit: Experiences with sustainable software. *CoRR*, abs/1309.1796, 2013.

[AL09]   Timo Aila and Samuli Laine. Understanding the efficiency of ray traversal on GPUs. In *Proceedings of High-Performance Graphics 2009*, pages 145–149, 2009.

[ALK12]   Timo Aila, Samuli Laine, and Tero Karras. Understanding the efficiency of ray traversal on GPUs – Kepler and Fermi addendum. NVIDIA Technical Report NVR-2012-02, NVIDIA Corporation, June 2012.

[Amd67]   Gene M. Amdahl. Validity of the single processor approach to achieving large scale computing capabilities. In *Proceedings of the April 18-20, 1967, Spring Joint Computer Conference*, AFIPS '67 (Spring), pages 483–485, New York, NY, USA, 1967. ACM.

[ASW13]   Marco Ament, Filip Sadlo, and Daniel Weiskopf. Ambient volume scattering. *IEEE Transactions on Visualization and Computer Graphics*, 19(12):2936–2945, 2013.

[AW13]   Stefan Auer and Rüdiger Westermann. Direct contouring of implicit closest point surfaces. In M.-A. Otaduy and O. Sorkine, editors, *EG 2013 - short papers*, pages 1–4. Eurographics Association, 2013.

[Bak77]   N.S. Bakhvalov. *Numerical methods: analysis, algebra, ordinary differential equations*. MIR Publishers, 1977.

[BCH12]   Wes E. Bethel, Hank Childs, and Charles Hansen. *High Performance Visualization—Enabling Extreme-Scale Scientific Insight*. Chapman & Hall, CRC Computational Science. CRC Press/Francis–Taylor Group, Boca Raton, FL, USA, November 2012.

[BEL⁺07]   Solomon Boulos, Dave Edwards, J. Dylan Lacewell, Joe Kniss, Jan Kautz, Peter Shirley, and Ingo Wald. Packet-based whitted and distribution ray tracing. In *GI '07: Proceedings of Graphics Interface 2007*. ACM, May 2007.

[Ben75]   Jon L Bentley. Multidimensional binary search trees used for associative searching. *Communications of the ACM*, 18(9):509–517, 1975.

[Bli77]   James F Blinn. Models of light reflection for computer synthesized pictures. In *SIGGRAPH '77: Proceedings of the 4th annual conference on Computer graphics and interactive techniques*, August 1977.

[Bli96]   Jim Blinn. *Jim Blinn's corner: a trip down the graphics pipeline*. Morgan Kaufmann Publishers Inc., San Francisco, CA, USA, 1996.

[BPT02]   Chandrajit Bajaj, Sangmin Park, and A. Thane. Parallel multi-pc volume rendering system. *CS & ICES Technical Report, University of Texas at Austin*, 2, 2002.

[BSF⁺91]   William J. Bolosky, Michael L. Scott, Robert P. Fitzgerald, Robert J. Fowler, and Alan L. Cox. NUMA policies and their relation to memory architecture. In *ASPLOS IV: Proceedings of the fourth international conference on Architectural support for programming languages and operating systems*. ACM, April 1991.

[Bus11]   Bussler, Michael and Rick, Tobias and Kelle-Emden, Andreas and Hentschel, Bernd and Kuhlen, Torsten. Interactive particle tracing in time-varying tetrahedral grids. In *Proceedings of the 11th Eurographics conference on Parallel Graphics and Visualization*, pages 71–80. Eurographics Association, 2011.

[BWW+01] Carsten Benthin, Ingo Wald, Sven Woop, Manfred Ernst, and William R. Mark. Combining single and packet ray tracing for arbitrary ray distributions on the intel(r) mic architecture. *IEEE Transactions on Visualization and Computer Graphics*, 2001.

[CBB+05] Hank Childs, Eric Brugger, Kathleen Bonnell, Jeremy Meredith, Mark Miller, Brad Whitlock, and Nelson Max. A contract based system for large data visualization. In *Visualization, 2005. VIS 05. IEEE*, pages 191–198. IEEE, 2005.

[CDE13] Biagio Cosenza, Carsten Dachsbacher, and Ugo Erra. GPU cost estimation for load balancing in parallel ray tracing. In *International Conference on Computer Graphics Theory and Applications (GRAPP)*, pages 139–151, 2013.

[CH02] Liviu Coconu and Hans-Christian Hege. Hardware-accelerated point-based rendering of complex scenes. In *EGRW '02: Proceedings of the 13th Eurographics workshop on Rendering*. Eurographics Association, July 2002.

[CJ05] Christopher S. Co and Kenneth I. Joy. Isosurface generation for large-scale scattered data visualization. In *Proceedings of Vision, Modeling and Visualization*, pages 233–240, 2005.

[Com14a] Commander, Darrell. libjpeg-turbo — main / libjpeg-turbo. http://www.libjpeg-turbo.org/Main/HomePage, 2014.

[Com14b] Commander, Darrell. Virtualgl — main / libjpeg-turbo. http://www.virtualgl.org, 2014.

[CRZP04] Wei Chen, Liu Ren, Matthias Zwicker, and Hanspeter Pfister. Hardware-accelerated adaptive EWA volume splatting. In *VIS '04: Proceedings of the conference on Visualization '04*. IEEE Computer Society, October 2004.

[CT82]   Robert L. Cook and Kenneth E. Torrance. A reflectance model for computer graphics. *ACM Transactions on Graphics (TOG)*, 1(1):7–24, January 1982.

[CT08]   Daniel Cederman and Philippas Tsigas. On dynamic load balancing on graphics processors. *Proceedings of the 23rd ACM SIGGRAPH/EUROGRAPHICS Symposium on Graphics Hardware*, pages 57–64, 2008.

[CVKG10]   Long Chen, Oreste Villa, Sriram Krishnamoorthy, and Guang R. Gao. Dynamic load balancing on single-and multi-GPU systems. *IEEE International Symposium on Parallel and Distributed Processing (IPDPS)*, pages 1–12, 2010.

[Des14]   DeskVOX. Deskvox volume explorer. https://github.com/deskvox/deskvox, 2014.

[DGBP05]   David E. DeMarle, Christiaan P. Gribble, Solomon Boulos, and Steven G. Parker. Memory sharing for interactive ray tracing on clusters. *Parallel Computing*, 31(2):221–242, 2005.

[DK12]   Aritra Dasgupta and Robert Kosara. The importance of tracing data through the visualization pipeline. In *Proceedings of the 2012 BELIV Workshop: Beyond Time and Errors-Novel Evaluation Methods for Visualization*, page 9. ACM, 2012.

[DKC+98]   Frank Dachille, Kevin Kreeger, Baoquan Chen, Ingmar Bitter, and Arie Kaufman. High-quality volume rendering using texture mapping hardware. *Proceedings of the ACM SIGGRAPH/EUROGRAPHICS workshop on Graphics hardware*, pages 69–ff., 1998.

[DM98]   Leonardo Dagum and Ramesh Menon. OpenMP: an industry standard API for shared-memory programming. *Computational Science & Engineering, IEEE*, 5(1):46–55, 1998.

[dSB04]   Selan dos Santos and Ken Brodlie. Gaining understanding of multi-
            variate and multidimensional data through visualization. *Computers
            & Graphics*, 28(3):311–325, 2004.

[EJR⁺13]   Tiago Etiene, Daniel Jonsson, Timo Ropinski, Carlos Scheidegger, Joao
            Comba, Luis Nonato, Robert Kirby, Anders Ynnerman, and Claudio
            Silva. Verifying Volume Rendering Using Discretization Error Analysis.
            Visualization and Computer Graphics, IEEE Transactions on, 20(99),
            2013.

[EKE01]   Klaus Engel, Martin Kraus, and Thomas Ertl. High-quality pre-
            integrated volume rendering using hardware-accelerated pixel shading.
            In *Proceedings of the ACM SIGGRAPH/EUROGRAPHICS Workshop
            on Graphics Hardware*, HWWS '01, pages 9–16, New York, NY, USA,
            2001. ACM.

[EP07]   Stefan Eilemann and Renato Pajarola. Direct send compositing for
            parallel sort-last rendering. In *EG PGV'07: Proceedings of the 7th
            Eurographics conference on Parallel Graphics and Visualization*. Euro-
            graphics Association, May 2007.

[EW92]   Rae Earnshaw and Norman Wiseman. *An introductory guide to scien-
            tific visualization*. Springer-Verlag, 1992.

[FBJ⁺08]   Nadeem Firasta, Mark Buxton, Paula Jinbo, Kaveh Nasri, and Shihjong
            Kuo. Intel avx: New frontiers in performance improvements and energy
            efficiency. *Intel White Paper*, 2008.

[FK10]   Thomas Fogal and Jens Krüger. Tuvok, an Architecture for Large Scale
            Volume Rendering. *Proceedings of the 15th International Workshop on
            Vision, Modeling, and Visualization*, pages 57–66, 2010.

[Fly72]   Michael J. Flynn. Some computer organizations and their effectiveness.
            IEEE Transactions on Computers, 21(9):948–960, September 1972.

[FvDFH90]   James D. Foley, Andries van Dam, Steven K. Feiner, and John F.
            Hughes. *Computer Graphics: Principles and Practice (2Nd Ed.)*.

Addison-Wesley Longman Publishing Co., Inc., Boston, MA, USA, 1990.

[Gol91]   David Goldberg. What every computer scientist should know about floating-point arithmetic. *ACM Comput. Surv.*, 23(1):5–48, March 1991.

[Goo14]   Google. snappy - a fast compressor/decompressor - google project hosting. `https://code.google.com/p/snappy/`, 2014.

[GSO12]   Kshitij Gupta, Jeff A. Stuart, and John D. Owens. A study of persistent threads style GPU programming for GPGPU workloads. *Innovative Parallel Computing (InPar), 2012*, pages 1–14, 2012.

[HAF⁺96]   William L. Hibbard, John Anderson, Ian Foster, Brian E. Paul, Chad Schafer, and Mary K. Tyree. Exploring coupled atmosphere-ocean models using Vis5D. *International Journal of High Performance Computing Applications*, 10(2):211–222, 1996.

[HAM06]   Jon Hasselgren and Tomas Akenine-Möller. Efficient depth buffer compression. In *EUROGRAPHICS Conference On Graphics Hardware: Proceedings of the 21 st ACM Eurographics symposium on Graphics hardware: Vienna, Austria*, pages 103–110, 2006.

[HÇE96]   Peter Hastreiter, Huseyin K. Çakmak, and Thomas Ertl. Intuitive and interactive manipulation of 3D data sets by integrating texture mapping based volume rendering into the openinventor class hierarchy. *Bildverarbeitung fuer die Medizin: Algorithmen, Systeme, Anwendungen*, pages 149–154, 1996.

[Hen04]   Amy Henderson. *The ParaView Guide: A Parallel Visualization Application*. Kitware, November 2004.

[HKRS⁺06]   Markus Hadwiger, Joe M. Kniss, Christof Rezk-Salama, Daniel Weiskopf, and Klaus Engel. *Real-time Volume Graphics*. A. K. Peters, Ltd., Natick, MA, USA, 2006.

[HLC91]   Robert B. Haber, Bruce Lucas, and Nancy S. Collins. A data model for
           scientific visualization with provisions for regular and irregular grids.
           In *IEEE Conference on Visualization, 1991.*, pages 298–305, 1991.

[HM90]   Robert B. Haber and David A. McNabb. Visualization idioms: a
           conceptual model for scientific visualization systems. *Visualization in
           Scientific Computing*, pages 74–93, 1990.

[HMS95]   Wolfgang Heidrich, Michael McCool, and John Stevens. Interactive
           maximum projection volume rendering. In *Visualization, 1995. Visual-
           ization '95. Proceedings., IEEE Conference on*, pages 11–18, 1995.

[HPS12]   High-performance scientific computing in terrestrial systems, HPSC
           TerrSys. http://www.hpsc-terrsys.de, 2012.

[HPvW94]   Lambertus Hesselink, Frits H. Post, and Jarke J. van Wijk. Research
           issues in vector and tensor field visualization. *IEEE Computer Graphics
           and Applications*, 14(2):76–79, March 1994.

[HTG08]   Quan Huynh-Thu and Mohammed Ghanbari. Scope of validity of PSNR
           in image/video quality assessment. *Electronics Letters*, 44(13):800,
           2008.

[IBH11]   Thiago Ize, Carson Brownlee, and Charles D. Hansen. Real-time ray
           tracer for visualizing massive models on a cluster. In *Eurographics
           Symposium on Parallel Graphics and Visualization*, 2011.

[Int13]   Intel®.   Intel® 64 and ia-32 architectures devel-
           oper's   manual: Vol.   2a.   http://www.intel.com/
           content/dam/www/public/us/en/documents/manuals/
           64-ia-32-architectures-software-developer-vol-2a-manual.
           pdf, September 2013.

[Int14]   Intel®. Intel®cilk^{TM} plus. http://software.intel.com/en-us/
           intel-cilk-plus, 2014.

[JH04]   Christopher Johnson and Charles D. Hansen. *Visualization Handbook*.
           Academic Press, Inc., Orlando, FL, USA, 2004.

[JR13]   James Jeffers and James Reinders. *Intel Xeon Phi Coprocessor High Performance Programming*. Elsevier Science & Technology Books, 2013.

[JvRLHK04] Thomas Jansen, Bartosz von Rymon-Lipinski, Nils Hanssen, and Erwin Keeve. Fourier volume rendering on the GPU using a split-stream-FFT. In *Vision, modeling, and visualization 2004: proceedings, November 16-18, 2004, Standford, USA*, page 395. IOS Press, 2004.

[KA97]   Hüseyin Kutluca and Cevdet Aykanat. Image-space decomposition algorithms for sort-first parallel volume rendering of unstructured grids. *The Journal of Supercomputing*, 15(1):51–93, 1997.

[KD98]   Gordon Kindlmann and James W. Durkin. Semi-automatic generation of transfer functions for direct volume rendering. In *Proceedings of the 1998 IEEE symposium on Volume visualization*, pages 79–86. ACM, 1998.

[Khr13]   Khronos™Group. OpenCL - the open standard for parallel programming of heterogeneous systems. `http://www.khronos.org/opencl/`, January 2013.

[Kit14a]   Kitware. ParaView - open source scientific visualization. `http://www.paraview.org`, 2014.

[Kit14b]   Kitware. Vtk - the visualization toolkit. `http://www.vtk.org`, 2014.

[KKC+13]   Rakesh Krishnaiyer, Emre Kultursay, Pankaj Chawla, Serguei Preis, Anatoly Zvezdin, and Hideki Saito. Compiler-based data prefetching and streaming non-temporal store generation for the intel(r) xeon phi(tm) coprocessor. In *IPDPS Workshops*, pages 1575–1586. IEEE, 2013.

[KLT07]   Jong Kwan Lee and Newman S. Timothy. New method for opacity correction in oversampled volume ray casting. *Journal of WSCG*, 15(1–3):1–8, 2007.

[KMM+01] Joe Kniss, Patrick McCormick, Allen McPherson, James Ahrens, James
          Painter, Alan Keahey, and Charles D. Hansen. Interactive texture-
          based volume rendering for large data sets. *Computer Graphics and
          Applications, IEEE*, 21(4):52–61, 2001.

[KOWT11] Tobias Klug, Michael Ott, Josef Weidendorfer, and Carsten Trinitis. Au-
          topin: automated optimization of thread-to-core pinning on multicore
          systems. In Per Stenström, editor, *Transactions on high-performance
          embedded architectures and compilers III*, Lecture Notes in Computer
          Science, pages 219–235. Springer-Verlag, Berlin, Heidelberg, 2011.

[KS13]   Martina Klose and Yaping Shao. Large-eddy simulation of turbulent
          dust emission. *Aeolian Research*, 8:49–58, 2013.

[KTW+11] Aaron Knoll, Sebastian Thelen, Ingo Wald, Charles D. Hansen, Hans
          Hagen, and Michael E. Papka. Full-resolution interactive CPU vol-
          ume rendering with coherent BVH traversal. *Pacific Visualization
          Symposium (PacificVis), 2011 IEEE*, pages 3–10, 2011.

[KVH84]   James T. Kajiya and Brian P. Von Herzen. Ray tracing volume densities.
          In *SIGGRAPH '84: Proceedings of the 11th annual conference on
          Computer graphics and interactive techniques*. ACM, January 1984.

[KW03]   Jens Krüger and Rüdiger Westermann. Acceleration techniques for
          GPU-based volume rendering. In *VIS '03: Proceedings of the 14th
          IEEE Visualization 2003 (VIS'03)*. IEEE Computer Society, October
          2003.

[LC87]   William Lorensen and Harvey Cline. Marching cubes: A high resolution
          3D surface construction algorithm. *SIGGRAPH '87: Proceedings of the
          14th annual conference on Computer graphics and interactive techniques*,
          1987.

[LCCK02] Joshua Leven, Jason Corso, Jonathan Cohen, and Subodh Kumar.
          Interactive visualization of unstructured grids using hierarchical 3D
          textures. In *Volume Visualization and Graphics, 2002. Proceedings.*

IEEE / ACM SIGGRAPH Symposium on, pages 37–44. IEEE Press, 2002.

[LCNC98]   Barthold Lichtenbelt, Randy Crane, Shaz Naqui, and Hewlett-Packard Company. *Introduction to Volume Rendering.* Hewlett-Packard Professional Books. Prentice Hall PTR, 1998.

[Lev88]   Marc Levoy. Display of surfaces from volume data. *IEEE Comput. Graph. Appl.*, 8(3):29–37, May 1988.

[LFTG97]   Eric P. F. Lafortune, Sing-Choong Foo, Kenneth E. Torrance, and Donald P. Greenberg. Non-linear approximation of reflectance functions. In *SIGGRAPH '97: Proceedings of the 24th annual conference on Computer graphics and interactive techniques.* ACM Press/Addison-Wesley Publishing Co., August 1997.

[LH91]   David Laur and Pat Hanrahan. Hierarchical splatting: a progressive refinement algorithm for volume rendering. *SIGGRAPH Comput. Graph.*, 25(4):285–288, July 1991.

[LL94]   Philippe Lacroute and Marc Levoy. Fast volume rendering using a shear-warp factorization of the viewing transformation. In *Computer Graphics Proceedings, Annual Conference Series*, 1994.

[LMHJ99]   Eric C. La Mar, Bernd Hamann, and Kenneth I. Joy. Multiresolution techniques for interactive texture-based volume visualization. In *Proceedings of the 10th IEEE Visualization 1999 Conference (VIS '99)*, VISUALIZATION '99, Washington, DC, USA, 1999. IEEE Computer Society.

[LMK03]   Wei Li, Klaus Mueller, and Arie Kaufman. Empty Space Skipping and Occlusion Clipping for Texture-based Volume Rendering. In *VIS '03: Proceedings of the 14th IEEE Visualization 2003 (VIS'03).* IEEE Computer Society, October 2003.

[lMPH94]   Kwan liu Ma, James S. Painter, and Charles D. Hansen. Parallel
            volume rendering using binary-swap compositing. *IEEE Computer
            Graphics and Applications*, 14:59–68, 1994.

[LNOM08]   Erik Lindholm, John Nickolls, Stuart Oberman, and John Montrym.
            NVIDIA Tesla: A unified graphics and computing architecture. *Micro,
            IEEE*, 28(2):39–55, 2008.

[LWK05]   John Leech, Paula Womack, and Phil Karlton. *OpenGL graphics with
            the X Window System*. Silicon Graphics, Mountain View, CA, USA,
            December 2005.

[MA04]   Kenneth Moreland and Edward Angel. A fast high accuracy volume
            renderer for unstructured data. In *Volume Visualization and Graphics,
            2004 IEEE Symposium on*, pages 9–16. IEEE, 2004.

[Ma09]   Kwan-Liu Ma. In situ visualization at extreme scale: Challenges and
            opportunities. *IEEE Computer Graphics and Applications*, 29:14–19,
            2009.

[Max95]   Nelson Max. Optical models for direct volume rendering. *IEEE
            Transactions on Visualization and Computer Graphics*, 1(2):99–108,
            June 1995.

[MCEF94]   Steven Molnar, Michael Cox, David Ellsworth, and Henry Fuchs. A
            sorting classification of parallel rendering. *IEEE Computer Graphics
            and Applications*, 14:23–32, 1994.

[MDBZ87]   Bruce Howard McCormick, Thomas A. DeFanti, Maxine D. Brown,
            and Raul Zaritsky. Visualization in Scientific Computing, 1987.

[MHK95]   Xiaoyang Mao, Lichan Hong, and Arie Kaufman. Splatting of curvilin-
            ear volumes. In *Visualization, 1995. Visualization '95. Proceedings.,
            IEEE Conference on*, pages 61–68, 1995.

[MIH04]   Manabu Matsui, Fumihiko Ino, and Kenichi Hagihara. Parallel volume
            rendering with early ray termination for visualizing large-scale datasets.

In *ISPA '04: Proceedings of the Second international conference on Parallel and Distributed Processing and Applications*. Springer-Verlag, December 2004.

[Mit07]   Martin Mittring. Finding next gen: Cryengine 2. In *ACM SIGGRAPH 2007 Courses*, SIGGRAPH '07, pages 97–121, New York, NY, USA, 2007. ACM.

[ML94]   Stephen R. Marschner and Richard Lobb. An evaluation of reconstruction filters for volume rendering. In R. Daniel Bergeron and Arie E. Kaufman, editors, *IEEE Visualization*, pages 100–107. IEEE Computer Society, 1994.

[MMD08]   Stéphane Marchesin, Catherine Mongenet, and Jean-Michel Dischler. Multi-GPU sort-last volume visualization. In *EG PGV '08: Proceedings of the 8th Eurographics conference on Parallel Graphics and Visualization*. Eurographics Association, April 2008.

[MMFE06]   Ricardo Marroquim, André Maximo, Ricardo Farias, and Claudio Esperança. GPU-based cell projection for interactive volume rendering. In *19th Brazilian Symposium on Computer Graphics and Image Processing, SIBGRAPI'06*, pages 147–154. IEEE, 2006.

[Mor09]   Kenneth Moreland. Diverging color maps for scientific visualization. In *Proceedings of the 5th International Symposium on Visual Computing*. Springer Berlin Heidelberg, December 2009.

[Mor13]   Kenneth Moreland. A Survey of Visualization Pipelines. *IEEE Transactions on Visualization and Computer Graphics*, 19(3):367–378, March 2013.

[MSRMH09]   Jennis Meyer-Spradow, Timo Ropinski, Jörg Mensmann, and Klaus Hinrichs. Voreen: A rapid-prototyping environment for ray-casting-based volume visualizations. *Computer Graphics and Applications, IEEE*, 29(6):6–13, 2009.

[Neu94]   Ulrich Neumann. Communication costs for parallel volume-rendering algorithms. *Computer Graphics and Applications, IEEE*, 14(4):49–58, 1994.

[NVI13]   NVIDIA®. CUDA C programming guide. `http://docs.nvidia.com/cuda/pdf/CUDA_C_Programming_Guide.pdf`, July 2013.

[ORM08]   Ryan Overbeck, Ravi Ramamoorthi, and William R. Mark. Large ray packets for real-time Whitted ray tracing. In *Interactive Ray Tracing, 2008. RT 2008. IEEE Symposium on*, pages 41–48, 2008.

[Pac11]   Peter Pacheco. *An Introduction to Parallel Programming*. Morgan Kaufmann Publishers Inc., San Francisco, CA, USA, 1st edition, 2011.

[PD84]   Thomas Porter and Tom Duff. Compositing digital images. *SIGGRAPH Comput. Graph.*, 18(3):253–259, January 1984.

[Per05]   Colin Percival. Cache missing for fun and profit. In *Proc. of BSDCan 2005*, 2005.

[Pfi01]   Gregory F. Pfister. An introduction to the InfiniBand architecture. *High Performance Mass Storage and Parallel I/O*, 42:617–632, 2001.

[PGR⁺09]   Tom Peterka, David Goodell, Robert Ross, Han-Wei Shen, and Rajeev Thakur. A configurable algorithm for parallel image-compositing applications. In *High Performance Computing Networking, Storage and Analysis, Proceedings of the Conference on*, pages 1–10. ACM, 2009.

[PH08]   David A. Patterson and John L. Hennessy. *Computer Organization and Design, Fourth Edition, Fourth Edition: The Hardware/Software Interface (The Morgan Kaufmann Series in Computer Architecture and Design)*. Morgan Kaufmann Publishers Inc., San Francisco, CA, USA, 4th edition, 2008.

[PHE⁺11]   Dawid Pajak, Robert Herzog, Elmar Eisemann, Karol Myszkowski, and Hans-Peter Seidel. Scalable Remote Rendering with Depth and Motion-flow Augmented Streaming. *Computer Graphics Forum*, March 2011.

[Pho75]   Bui Tuong Phong. Illumination for computer generated pictures. *Graphics and Image Processing*, 18(6):311–317, 1975.

[Pin88]   Juan Pineda. A parallel algorithm for polygon rasterization. *ACM SIGGRAPH Computer Graphics*, 22(4):17–20, 1988.

[PRY+08]   Tom Peterka, Robert Ross, Hongfeng Yu, Kwan-Liu Ma, Wesley Kendall, and Jian Huang. Assessing improvements to the parallel volume rendering pipeline at large scale. *Proceedings of SC 08 Ultrascale Visualization Workshop*, pages 13–23, 2008.

[Qt 14]   Qt Project. Qt project. `http://qt-project.org`, 2014.

[RBB+11]   Marc Ruiz, Anton Bardera, Imma Boada, Ivan Viola, Miquel Feixas, and Mateu Sbert. Automatic transfer functions based on informational divergence. *IEEE Transactions on Visualization and Computer Graphics*, 17(12):1932–1941, 2011.

[RLL+96]   Dirk Rantzau, Ulrich Lang, Ruth Lang, Harald Nebel, Andreas Wierse, and Roland Rühle. Collaborative and interactive visualization in a distributed high performance software environment. In M. Chen, P. Townsend, and J.A. Vince, editors, *High Performance Computing for Computer Graphics and Visualisation*, pages 207–216. Springer London, 1996.

[Roe14]   Roelofs, Greg. libpng home page. `http://www.libpng.org/pub/png/libpng.html`, 2014.

[Ros09]   Rost, Randi J. and Licea-Kane, Bill and Ginsburg, Dan and Kessenich, John M. and Lichtenbelt, Barthold and Malan, Hugh and Weiblen, Mike. *OpenGL Shading Language*. Addison-Wesley Professional, 3rd edition, 2009.

[RSFWH98] Tristan Richardson, Quentin Stafford-Fraser, Kenneth R. Wood, and Andy Hopper. Virtual network computing. *Internet Computing, IEEE*, 2(1):33–38, 1998.

[RSK05]   Christof Rezk-Salama and Andreas Kolb. A vertex program for effi-
            cient box-plane intersection. *Proc. Vision, Modeling and Visualization
            (VMV)*, pages 115–122, 2005.

[RV06]   Daniel Ruijters and Anna Vilanova. Optimizing GPU volume rendering.
            Journal of WSCG, 14(1-3):9–16, 2006.

[SC05]   Daniel Steinberg and Stuart Cheshire. *Zero configuration networking:
            the definitive guide.* O'Reilly Media, Inc., 2005.

[Sch97]   Dieter Schmalstieg. *The remote rendering pipeline - managing geometry
            and bandwidth in distributed virtual environments.* PhD thesis, Vienna
            University of Technology, November 1997.

[Sch03]   Jürgen P. Schulze. *Interactive Volume Rendering in Virtual Environ-
            ments.* PhD thesis, University of Stuttgart, August 2003.

[SCK11]   Heung-Yeung Shum, Shing-Chow Chan, and Sing Bing Kang. *Image-
            Based Rendering.* Springer, 2011.

[SGC01]   Dave Sager, Desktop Platforms Group, and Intel Corp. The microar-
            chitecture of the pentium 4 processor. *Intel Technology Journal*, 1:2001,
            2001.

[SGHS98]   Jonathan Shade, Steven Gortler, Li-wei He, and Richard Szeliski.
            Layered depth images. In *SIGGRAPH '98: Proceedings of the 25th
            annual conference on Computer graphics and interactive techniques.*
            ACM, July 1998.

[She03]   Jonathan Richard Shewchuk. Updating and constructing constrained
            delaunay and constrained regular triangulations by flips. In *SCG '03:
            Proceedings of the nineteenth annual symposium on Computational
            geometry.* ACM, June 2003.

[SK00]   Heung-Yeung Shum and Sing Bing Kang. A review of image-based
            rendering techniques. In *Visual Communications and Image Processing*,
            pages 1–12, June 2000.

[SK10]   Jason Sanders and Edward Kandrot. *CUDA by Example: An Introduction to General-Purpose GPU Programming*. Addison-Wesley Professional, 1 edition, July 2010.

[SL02]   Jürgen P. Schulze and Ulrich Lang. The parallelization of the perspective shear-warp volume rendering algorithm. In *EGPGV '02: Proceedings of the Fourth Eurographics Workshop on Parallel Graphics and Visualization*. Eurographics Association, September 2002.

[SME02]   Simon Stegmaier, Marcelo Magallón, and Thomas Ertl. *A generic solution for hardware-accelerated remote visualization*. Eurographics Association, May 2002.

[SML06]   Will Schroeder, Ken Martin, and Bill Lorensen. *Visualization Toolkit: An Object-Oriented Approach to 3D Graphics, 4th Edition*. Kitware, 4th edition, December 2006.

[SNL01]   Jürgen P. Schulze, Roland Niemeier, and Ulrich Lang. The perspective shear-warp algorithm in a virtual environment. In *Proceedings of the Conference on Visualization '01*, VIS '01, pages 207–214, Washington, DC, USA, 2001. IEEE Computer Society.

[SRC10]   Toby Sharp, Duncan Robertson, and Antonio Criminisi. Volume rendering on server GPUs for enterprise-scale medical applications. Technical Report 72, Microsoft Research, Cambridge, UK, Microsoft Research, Cambridge, UK, 2010.

[SSC02]   Mel Slater, Anthony Steed, and Yiorgos Chrysanthou. *Computer Graphics and Virtual Environments: From Realism to Real-time*. Addison-Wesley, 2002.

[ST90]   Peter Shirley and Allan Tuchman. A polygonal approximation to direct scalar volume rendering. In *San Diego Workshop on Volume Visualization*, pages 63–70. ACM, 1990.

[Ste98]   W. Richard Stevens. *UNIX Network Programming: Interprocess communications*. The Unix Networking Reference Series , Vol 2. Prentice Hall PTR, 1998.

[SWWL01]   Jürgen P. Schulze, Uwe Wössner, SP Walz, and Ulrich Lang. Volume rendering in a virtual environment. In *Immersive Projection Technology and Virtual Environments 2001: proceedings of the Eurographics Workshop in Stuttgart, Germany, May 16-18, 2001*, page 187, 2001.

[TL93]   Takashi Totsuka and Marc Levoy. Frequency domain volume rendering. In *Proceedings of the 20th annual conference on Computer graphics and interactive techniques*, pages 271–278. ACM, 1993.

[TYRG+06]   Tiankai Tu, Hongfeng Yu, Leonardo Ramirez-Guzman, Jacobo Bielak, Omar Ghattas, Kwan-Liu Ma, and David R. O'Hallaron. From mesh generation to scientific visualization: An end-to-end approach to parallel supercomputing. In *Proceedings of the ACM/IEEE SC 2006 Conference*, 2006.

[Uni06]   Universität Erlangen. The volume library. http://www9.informatik. uni-erlangen.de/External/vollib/, 2006.

[Vis11]   VisPME, BMBF-No.: 01IH08009B. http://vis.uni-koeln.de/ vispme.html?&L=1, 2011.

[Vis14]   VisIt. Main page - visitusers.org. http://www.visitusers.org, 2014.

[VKG04]   Ivan Viola, Armin Kanitsar, and Meister Eduard Gröller. GPU-based frequency domain volume rendering. In *SCCG '04: Proceedings of the 20th spring conference on Computer graphics*, April 2004.

[VWE05]   Joachim E. Vollrath, Daniel Weiskopf, and Thomas Ertl. A generic software framework for the GPU volume rendering pipeline. *Proc. Vision, Modeling and Visualization*, pages 391–398, 2005.

[Wal11]   Ingo Wald. Active thread compaction for GPU path tracing. In *Proceedings of High Performance Graphics 2011*, 2011.

[War92]   Gregory J. Ward. Measuring and modeling anisotropic reflection. In *SIGGRAPH '92: Proceedings of the 19th annual conference on Computer graphics and interactive techniques*. ACM, July 1992.

[WE98]   Rüdiger Westermann and Thomas Ertl. Efficiently using graphics hardware in volume rendering applications. In *SIGGRAPH '98: Proceedings of the 25th annual conference on Computer graphics and interactive techniques*. ACM, July 1998.

[Wer93]   Josie Wernecke. *The Inventor Mentor: Programming Object-Oriented 3d Graphics with Open Inventor, Release 2*. Addison-Wesley Longman Publishing Co., Inc., Boston, MA, USA, 1st edition, 1993.

[Wes89]   Lee Westover. Interactive volume rendering. In *VVS '89: Proceedings of the 1989 Chapel Hill workshop on Volume Visualization*, pages 9–16. ACM, May 1989.

[Wes90]   Lee Westover. Footprint evaluation for volume rendering. In *SIGGRAPH '90: Proceedings of the 17th annual conference on Computer graphics and interactive techniques*. ACM, September 1990.

[WKP11]   Craig M. Wittenbrink, Emmett Kilgariff, and Arjun Prabhu. Fermi GF100 GPU architecture. *Micro, IEEE*, 31(2), 2011.

[WSB01]   Ingo Wald, Philipp Slusallek, and Carsten Benthin. Interactive distributed ray tracing of highly complex models. In *Rendering Techniques 2001 - Proceedings of the 12th EUROGRAPHICS Workshop on Rendering*, pages 274–285, 2001.

[WSBW01]   Ingo Wald, Philipp Slusallek, Carsten Benthin, and Markus Wagner. Interactive rendering with coherent ray tracing. *Computer Graphics Forum (Proceedings of EUROGRAPHICS)*, 20(3):153–164, 2001.

[YWM08]   Hongfeng Yu, Chaoli Wang, and Kwan-Liu Ma. Massively parallel volume rendering using 2-3 swap image compositing. In *SC '08: Proceedings of the 2008 ACM/IEEE conference on Supercomputing*, pages 1–11. IEEE Press, August 2008.

[ZAL12]   Stefan Zellmann, Martin Aumüller, and Ulrich Lang. Image-Based Re-
           mote Real-Time Volume Rendering - Decoupling Rendering from View
           Point Updates. In *Proceedings of the ASME 2012 International Design
           Engineering Technical Conferences & Computers and Information in
           Engineering Conference*. ASME, 12 -15 August 2012.

[ZL12]   Stefan Zellmann and Ulrich Lang. A Software Architecture for Dis-
           tributed Volume Rendering on HPC Systems. In *Proceedings of the
           24th IASTED International Conference on Parallel and Distributed
           Computing and Systems*, pages 94–101. IASTED, 12 -14 November
           2012.

[ZL13]   Stefan Zellmann and Ulrich Lang. A Comparison of GPU Box-Plane
           Intersection Algorithms for Direct Volume Rendering. In *Proceedings
           of the 14th IASTED International Conference on Computer Graphics
           and Imaging*, pages 153–160, February 2013.

[ZM13]   Yubo Zhang and Kwan-Liu Ma. Lighting design for globally illuminated
           volume rendering. *IEEE Transactions on Visualization and Computer
           Graphics*, 19(12):2946–2955, 2013.

[ZPvBG01] Matthias Zwicker, Hanspeter Pfister, Jereon van Baar, and Markus
           Gross. EWA volume splatting. In *Visualization, 2001. VIS '01. Pro-
           ceedings*, pages 29–538, 2001.

[ZT09]   Jianlong Zhou and Masahiro Takatsuka. Automatic transfer func-
           tion generation using contour tree controlled residue flow model and
           color harmonics. *IEEE Transactions on Visualization and Computer
           Graphics*, 15(6):1481–1488, 2009.

www.ingramcontent.com/pod-product-compliance
Lightning Source LLC
Chambersburg PA
CBHW021043210326
41598CB00016B/1099